EXCELLENCE ILLUSTRATED

CROSSTRAINING
PUBLISHING

By Dr. Elliot Johnson

Introduction to . . .

EXCELLENCE ILLUSTRATED!

WHAT IS EXCELLENCE? Webster says it is "the fact or condition of excelling; superiority, surpassing goodness or merit."

An unknown author — one who sounds much like a coach — says excellence is:

"Preparing more than others care to or expect, practicing more often than the average person believes is necessary, believing in the quality of every moment and every day — this is what excellence is all about.

And it comes from striving, maintaining the highest standards, the highest beliefs, looking after the smallest detail, using the basics, and going the extra mile. Excellence means caring — caring enough about making a difference. It means making a special effort to do more than is asked and to expect more of oneself."

It is for motivation to excellence in life that this book is written. May your spirit be lifted to the excellence that is found in Christ Jesus!

Elliot Johnson

Contents

Excellence Illustrated by Examples • 9

Excellence Illustrated by Humor • 91

Excellence Illustrated

with Object Lessons • 113

EXCELLENCE ILLUSTRATED
By Examples

*— consider the outcome of their way
of life and imitate their faith —*
Hebrews 13:7

A Positive Mind-set

Whether You Think You Can Or You Can't — You're Probably Right

If you think you are beaten, you are;
If you think that you dare not, you don't;
If you'd like to win, but you think you can't,
It's almost certain you won't.

If you think you'll lose, you've lost;
For out in the world you'll find
Success begins with a fellow's will.
It's all in the state of mind.

If you think you are outclassed, you are;
You've got to think high to rise;
You've got to be sure of yourself before
You can ever win a prize.

Life's battles don't always go
To the stronger or faster man;
But sooner or later the man who wins
Is the man who thinks he can.

– Author Unknown

Question:

Do you go through life with a positive mind-set?

Excellence from Philippians 4:8

> — *if anything is excellent or praiseworthy* — *think about such things.*

11

Adopt A Winning Attitude

Winners vs Losers

When a winner makes a mistake, he says, "I was wrong;"
When a loser makes a mistake, he says, "It wasn't my fault."

A winner works harder than a loser and has more time;
A loser is always "too busy" to do what is necessary.

A winner goes through a problem;
A loser goes around it, and never gets past it.

A winner makes commitments;
A loser makes promises.

A winner says, "I'm good, but not as good as I ought to be;"
A loser says, "I'm not as bad as a lot of other people."

A winner listens;
A loser just waits until it's his turn to talk.

A winner respects those who are superior to him and tries to learn something from them;
A loser resents those who are superior to him and tries to find chinks in their armor.

A winner feels responsible for more than his job;
A loser says, "I only work here."

A winner says, "There ought to be a better way to do it;"
A loser says, "That's the way it's always been done here."
> – Pat Williams
> NBA General Manager and Vice President

Question:
Do you have the attitude of a winner or a loser?

Excellence from Ephesians 4:23

> *Be made new in the attitude of your minds.*

Appreciate Obstacles

IN THE NORTHEASTERN UNITED STATES, codfish are a big commercial business. There is a market for eastern cod all over, especially in sections farthest removed from the northeast coastline. But the public demand posed a problem to the shippers. At first they froze the cod, then shipped them elsewhere, but the freeze took away much of the flavor. So they experimented with shipping them alive, in tanks of sea water, but that proved even worse. Not only was it more expensive, the cod still lost its flavor and in addition, became soft and mushy. The texture was seriously affected.

Finally, some creative person solved the problem in a most innovative manner. The codfish were placed in the tank of water along with their natural enemy — the catfish. From the time the cod left the East Coast until it arrived at its westernmost destination, those ornery catfish chased the cod all over the tank. And, you guessed it, when the cod arrived at the market, they were as fresh as when they were first caught. There was no loss of flavor nor was the texture affected. If anything, it was better than before.

Each one of us is in a tank of particular and inescapable circumstances. It is painful enough to stay in the tank. But in addition to our situation, there are God-appointed "catfish" to bring sufficient tension that keeps us alive, alert, fresh and growing. It's all part of God's project to shape our character so we will be more like his Son. Understand why the catfish are in your tank. Understand they are part of God's method of producing character in your life and mine.

– Charles Swindoll

Question:
Who or what is the "catfish" in your life?

Excellence from Ephesians 5:20

> . . .always giving thanks to God the Father for every-
> thing, in the name of our Lord Jesus Christ.

Avoid Guessing About Life

ONLY ON RARE OCCASIONS does a hitter guess successfully what a pitcher will throw. He is a far better hitter if he constantly expects a fast ball and adjusts his swing if a curve or off-speed pitch is thrown. It's fundamental that the pitcher and catcher can "outguess" a hitter.

It's also fundamental that man can't "outguess" God. Man always loses when he tries. The Greeks used to say, "The dice of the gods are loaded." Even in their ignorance of the true God, they recognized man's limitations.

We cannot guess what God will do next. He is sovereign and omniscient (all-knowing). We are better off to follow Him by faith, trusting in His goodness. We dare not presume upon the future, We certainly dare not presume upon God!

Most importantly, we dare not guess whether or not we will spend eternity in heaven or in hell! If we don't *know* we'll go to heaven, we're probably headed for hell! The stakes are too high to guess about our eternal future. God has made it clear that we can know where we stand. We dare not trust our own works, our religion, or our philosophy of life. Christ is God's only sure way of salvation.

Question:

Are you guessing about life or do you know where you'll spend eternity?

Excellence from 1 John 5:12-13

He who has the Son has life; he who does not have the Son of God does not have life. I write these things to you who believe in the name of the Son of God so that you may know that you have eternal life.

14

Be A Good Father

I've Just Got To Be Successful As That Little Fella's Dad

I may never be as clever as my neighbor down the street.
I may never be as wealthy as some other men I meet.
I may never have the glory that some other men have had,
But I've just got to be successful as that little fella's dad.

There are certain dreams I cherish that I'd like to see come true,
And there are things that I'd accomplish before my working time
is through.
But the task my heart is set on is to guide a little lad,
And make myself successful as that little fella's dad.

Oh, I may never come to glory and I may never gather gold,
And men may count me as a failure
when my business life is told.
But if he who follows after shall be manly, then I'll be glad.
Because I'll know I've been successful as that little fella's dad.

It's the one job that I dream of, it's the task I think of most.
For if I fail that little fella, I have nothing else to boast.
For the wealth and fame I'd gather, all my fortune would be sad
If I fail to be successful as that little fella's dad.

— Author Unknown

Question:

Are you raising your sons to know God, to be manly, and
to love others?

Excellence from Colossians 3:21

*Fathers, do not embitter your children, or they will
become discouraged.*

15

Be A Good Sportsman

Dear Lord: In the battle that goes on through life
I ask but a field that is fair.
A chance that is equal with all in the strife,
A courage to strive and to dare.
And if I should win let it be by my code
With my faith and honor held high,
But teach me to stand by the side of the road
And cheer as the winners go by.

So grant me to conquer if conquer I can
By proving my worth in the fray,
But teach me to lose like a regular man
And not like a coward I pray.
Let me take of my lot of the warriors who strove
To victory splendid and high,
But teach me to stand by the side of the road
And cheer as the winners go by.

And Lord, let my shouts be ungrudging and clear
A tribute that comes from the heart,
And let me not cherish a snarl or a sneer
Nor play a sniveling part.
Let me say "there they ride," on whom laurels bestowed
For they played the game better than I.
Yes, teach me to stand by the side of the road
And cheer as the winners go by.

— Author Unknown

Question:

Are you a good sport?

Excellence from Luke 6:31

Do to others as you would have them do to you.

Be Careful What You Watch
The Devil's Vision

The devil once said to his demons below,
"Our work is progressing entirely too slow.
The holiness people stand in our way
Since they do not believe in the show or the play.
They teach that the carnival, circus and dance,
The tavern and honky-tonk with game of chance,
Drinking and smoking, these things are all wrong;
That Christians don't mess with the ungodly throng;
They are quick to condemn everything that we do
To cause unbelievers to be not a few.
They claim that these things are all of the devil;
That Christian folks live on a much higher level.
Now, fellows, their theology, while perfectly true
Is blocking the work we are trying to do.
We will have to get busy and figure a plan
That will change their standards as fast as we can.
Now I have a vision of just what we can do,
Harken, I'll tell this deception to you;
Then find ye a wise, but degenerate man
Whom I can use to help work out this plan.
There's nothing so real as the things that you see;
The eyes and the mind and the heart will agree;
So what can be better than an object to view?
I say, it will work and convince not a few.
The home is the place for this sinful device,
The people deceived will think it quite nice.
The world will possess it, most Christians can't tell
That it is all of the devil and plotted in hell!
We'll sell them with pictures of the latest news
And while they are looking, we'll advertise booze.
At first it will shock them; they'll seem in a daze,
But soon they'll be hardened and continue to gaze.
We'll give them some gospel that isn't too strong
And a few sacred songs to string them along.
They'll take in the ads, with the latest of fashions
And soon watch the shows that will stir evil passions.

17

Murder and love-making scenes they'll behold
Until their souls will be utterly cold.
The old family altar which once held such charm
Will soon lose its place without much alarm.
Praying in secret will also be lost
As they look at the screen without counting the cost.
The compromise preachers, who don't take their stand,
Will embrace this new vision and think it is grand.
They'll help fool the people and cause them to sin
By seeking this evil and taking it in.
Influence is great and this you can see;
Just look at my fall and you'll have to agree.
It won't take too long, my demons, to tell
That the vision of Satan will populate hell!
Divorce will increase, sex crimes will abound;
Much innocent blood will be spilled on the ground.
The home will be damned in short order I say.
When this vision of mine comes in to stay.
Get busy, my cohorts, and put this thing out;
We'll see if the church can continue to shout.
The holiness people who stand in our way
Will soon hush their crying against show and play.
We'll cover the earth with this devil vision
Then we'll camouflage it with the name television.
The people will think they are getting a treat
Till the antichrist comes and takes over his seat.
He'll rule the world while the viewers behold
The face of the beast, to whom they were sold.
We'll win through deception, this cannot fail;
Though some holiness preachers against it will rail."

— Author Unknown

Question:

Is television taking too much of your time? Does what you watch dull your spirit towards God?

Excellence from Psalm 101:3

I will set before my eyes no vile thing. The deeds of faithless men I hate; they will not cling to me.

Believe in Someone Else

JOHNNY ECHOLS AND MARTY MARION were boyhood friends who loved baseball. They made a pact to always play together, regardless of circumstances.

As time went on Johnny became quite good. He was soon the star of the team and the talk of Atlanta. One day the coach called Johnny aside and told him about the upcoming tryouts for the minor leagues. Johnny said, "That's great. Marty and I will sign up right away."

But the coach responded, "Don't worry about Marty. He's just an ugly duckling — too skinny, too slow, can't field, and can't hit." When Johnny told Marty's mom of his plans, Marty's mother also tried to discourage Johnny from including Marty. "He just won't make it," she said.

But Johnny's response was, "I know he can make it if he has a chance. He's got determination. He can learn to field and hit."

So they both tried out. But the training camp resulted in a contract for Johnny, and Marty being cut.

The minor league coach echoed the others to Johnny, "Leave your buddy. You've got great natural talent and potential."

Yet Johnny remained steadfast. "It's both of us or neither." And he left the camp.

The coach couldn't believe such loyalty, and days later he finally called both boys and offered them contracts.

Motivated by his friend's actions, Marty became deeply inspired and slowly began to improve. During their third year in the minor leagues Johnny washed out and quit. Marty became the rising star. Marty was called up to the majors for the St. Louis Cardinals as a shortstop. He became the team leader of what became a baseball dynasty in the 1940s called the Gas

House Gang. And in 1944 when they won the World Series, Marty Marion was named the Most Valuable Player.

Years earlier Marty's mom had asked Johnny, "Why are you so determined to keep this pact?" Johnny replied, "Belief is a kind of love. I believe in Marty. We're friends. Believing in someone is the best kind of love."

Question:
Who could you help in a great way by simply believing in him?

Excellence from 1 Corinthians 13:7

Love always protects, always trusts, always hopes, always perseveres.

Change Your World for Good

SIX DAYS BEFORE HE DIED, John Wesley wrote his last document. It was directed to a young Christian in Parliament named William Wilberforce. Though written 200 years ago, it has relevance to the task before American Christians today.
Wesley wrote:

> Unless God has raised you up for this very thing you will be worn out by the opposition of men and devils. But if God be for you, who can be against you.

Wilberforce faced a seemingly impossible task in challenging the slave trade. Public opinion was overwhelmingly against him; powerfully vested economic interests opposed and slandered him at every turn.

Wilberforce and his associates, who became known as the Clapham Sect, continued their battle for twenty years. Though they designed a masterful campaign, they never lost sight of Who was in charge; they devoted three hours of every day to prayer. When victory came at last, in 1807, it came not through the endeavors of mere men but by the sovereign accomplishment of Almighty God. And their work led not only to abolition of the slave trade, but it kindled a mighty spiritual awakening which lasted half a century.

Question:

What can you do to change things in America?

Excellence from Romans 8:31

> *If God is for us, who can be against us?*

Choose Words Carefully

IN A COUNTRY CHURCH of a small village an altar boy serving the priest at Sunday Mass accidentally dropped the cruet of wine. The village priest struck the altar boy sharply on the cheek and in a gruff voice shouted: "Leave the altar and don't come back!" That boy became Tito, the Communist leader.

In the cathedral of a large city an altar boy serving the bishop at Sunday Mass accidentally dropped the cruet of wine. With a warm twinkle in his eyes the bishop gently whispered: "Someday you will be a priest." That boy grew up to become Archbishop Fulton Sheen.

— Illustrations Unlimited

Question:
How many lives have you affected by the power of your words?

Excellence from James 3:2

We all stumble in many ways. If anyone is never at fault in what he says, he is a perfect man, able to keep his whole body in check.

Commitment I

The Fellowship of the Unashamed

I AM A PART OF THE FELLOWSHIP OF THE UNASHAMED. The dye has been cast. The decision has been made. I have stepped over the line. I won't look back, let up, slow down, or back away.

My past is redeemed, my present makes sense, my future is secure. I'm finished and done with low living, sight walking, small planning, smooth knees, colorless dreams, tamed visions, mundane talking, cheap giving, and dwarfed goals.

I no longer need pre-eminence, prosperity, position, promotions, plaudits, or popularity. I don't have to be right, first, tops, recognized, praised, regarded, or rewarded. I now live by faith, lean on His presence, walk with patience, live by prayer, and labor with power.

My face is set, my gait is fast, my goal is Heaven, my road is narrow, my way is rough, my companions are few, my Guide is reliable, my mission is clear. I cannot be bought, compromised, detoured, lured away, turned back, deluded, or delayed. I will not flinch in the face of sacrifice, hesitate in the presence of the adversary, negotiate at the table of the enemy, ponder at the pool of popularity, or meander in the maze of mediocrity.

I won't give up, shut up, let up, until I have stayed up, stored up, prayed up, paid up, spoken up for the cause of Christ. I am a disciple of Jesus Christ. I must go till He comes, give till I drop, preach till all know, and work till He stops me. And when He comes for His own, He will have no problem recognizing me. My banner is clear. I am a part of the fellowship of the unashamed.

— Author Unknown

Question:

Are you an unashamed follower of Jesus Christ?

Excellence from Romans 1:16

I am not ashamed of the gospel, because it is the power of God for the salvation of everyone who believes.

Commitment II

THREE HUNDRED YEARS BEFORE CHRIST, Alexander the Great conquered almost all of the known world using military strength, cleverness and a bit of diplomacy. One day Alexander and a small company of soldiers approached a strongly fortified walled city. Standing outside the walls, Alexander raised his voice and demanded to see the king. When the king arrived, Alexander insisted that the king surrender the city and its inhabitants to him and his little band of fighting men.

The king laughed, "Why should I surrender to you? You can't do us any harm!' But Alexander offered to give the king a demonstration. He ordered his men to line up single file and start marching. He marched them straight toward a sheer cliff.

The townspeople gathered on the wall and watched in shocked silence as, one by one, Alexander's soldiers marched without hesitation right off the cliff to their deaths! After ten soldiers died, Alexander ordered the rest of the men to return to his side. The townspeople and the king immediately surrendered to Alexander the Great. They realized that if a few men were actually willing to commit suicide at the command of this dynamic leader, then nothing could stop his eventual victory.

Think how much power Christ could demonstrate in your city with just a portion of such commitment to Himself.

Question:

Are you as committed to the ruler of the universe, Jesus Christ, as Alexander's soldiers were to him?

Excellence from Psalm 37:5-6

Commit your way to the LORD; trust in him and he will do this: He will make your righteousness shine like the dawn, the justice of your cause like the noon-day sun.

Consider Essentials Now

RUSSIAN NOVELIST LEO TOLSTOY told of an aunt who hurt him
deeply when she didn't take time to answer some questions
that were troubling him. She stirred his emotions by telling
him of Jesus' crucifixion, but when he cried out, "Auntie, why
did they torture Him?" she said simply, "They were wicked."
"But wasn't he God," Tolstoy asked. Instead of explaining that
Jesus was indeed God, that He had become a man so He
could die for our sins, she said, "Be still — it's 9 o'clock!"
When he persisted, she retorted, "Be quiet, I say, I'm going to
the dining room to have tea." This left young Tolstoy greatly
agitated. He couldn't comprehend that Jesus had been tor-
tured and his aunt was not interested enough to postpone her
tea time to discuss it with him.

Question:

Is your tea time (or your "tee" time) keeping you from
considering the important issues of life?

Excellence from Matthew 16:26

*What good will it be for a man if he gains the whole
world, yet forfeits his soul?*

Endure Tribulation

Strong in the Broken Places

A YOUNG FOOTBALL PLAYER suffered a broken leg in a game. It was a compound fracture and the youth underwent extensive surgery to set the bones in place. When the doctor came out of the operating room to see the player's parents and his coach, he assured them that the young man would again be able to play ball, though it would take much time and rehabilitation.

The boy's father asked whether this severe break would be subject to another fracture. The physician replied, "He will never break his leg again in that spot. The broken places, once healed, are always stronger than any other part."

Question:

What part of your life needs the healing touch of the Great Physician?

Excellence from Isaiah 61:1

He has sent me (Jesus) to bind up the brokenhearted, to proclaim freedom for the captives and release from darkness for the prisoners . . .

Excellence

I OWE ALMOST EVERYTHING TO FOOTBALL, which I spent the greater part of my life in, and I have never lost my respect, my admiration nor my love for what I consider a great game. Each Sunday after the battle, one group savors victory, another group wallows in the bitterness of defeat. The many hurts seem a small price to pay for having won and there is no reason at all which is adequate for having lost.

For the winner there is 100 percent elation, 100 percent laughter, 100 percent fun and for the loser the only thing left is a 100 percent resolution and 100 percent determination. The game, I think, is a great deal like life. Every man makes his own personal commitment toward excellence and toward victory. Although you know ultimate victory can never be completely won, it must be pursued with all of one's might and each week there is a new encounter, each year a new challenge.

All of the rings and all of the money and all of the color and all of the display, they linger only in a memory. But the spirit, the will to win, the will to excel, these are the things that endure and these are the qualities, of course, that are so much more important than any of the events that occur.

I'd like to say that the quality of any man's life is a full measure of that man's personal commitment to excellence and to victory, regardless of what field he may be in.

– Vince Lombardi

Question:
How is excellence related to your walk with Jesus Christ?

Excellence from Colossians 3:23

Whatever you do, work at it with all your heart, as working for the Lord, not for men.

27

Find An Encouraging Church

SEVERAL YEARS AGO studies were conducted among former American prisoners of war to determine what methods used by the enemy had been most effective in breaking their spirit. The findings revealed that they did not break down from physical deprivation and torture as quickly as they did from solitary confinement or from disrupted friendships caused by frequent changing of personnel. Attempts to get the prisoners divided in their attitudes toward one another proved to be the most successful method of discouraging them. It was further learned that the soldiers were not sustained primarily by faith in their country or by the rightness of the cause for which they fought. They drew their greatest strength from the close attachments to the small military units to which they belonged.

– M. R. De Haan II

Question:

Do you have a group (church) to which you are an encouragement and from which you receive encouragement?

Motivation from Hebrews 10:24-25

And let us consider how we may spur one another on toward love and good deeds. Let us not give up meeting together, as some are in the habit of doing, but let us encourage one another — and all the more as you see the Day approaching.

Flee From Sin

RADIO PERSONALITY PAUL HARVEY tells the story of how an Eskimo kills a wolf. The account is grisly, yet it offers fresh insight into the consuming, self-destructive nature of sin.

"First the Eskimo coats his knife blade with animal blood and allows it to freeze. Then he adds another layer of blood, and another, until the blade is completely concealed by frozen blood.

"Next, the hunter fixes his knife in the ground with the blade up. When a wolf follows his sensitive nose to the source of the scent and discovers the bait he licks it, tasting the fresh-frozen blood. He begins to lick faster, more and more vigorously, lapping the blade until the keen edge is bare. Feverishly now, harder and harder the wolf licks the blade in the Arctic night. So great becomes his craving for blood that the wolf does not notice the razor sharp sting of the naked blade on his tongue nor does he recognize the instant at which his insatiable thirst is being satisfied by his own warm blood. His carnivorous appetite just craves more — until the dawn finds him dead in the snow!"

Question:

Do you flee from the self-destruction of sinful practices.

Excellence from Romans 6:23

For the wages of sin is death . . .

Forgive

ARRESTED BY THE COMMUNISTS during the Korean war, a Christian from South Korea was sentenced to die before a firing squad. But when the officer in charge discovered the man headed an orphanage, he changed the order. Instead, he forced the believer to watch his 19-year-old son being shot dead in his place.

Later, the communist officer was captured by United Nations forces, tried, and condemned to die. But the Christian whose son had been killed made an emotional plea on behalf of the officer, asking that he be released into his custody. His request was granted and eventually the officer was converted to Christ and became a pastor!

Question:

Can the love of God allow you to forgive those who have wronged you?

Excellence from Matthew 6:12

Forgive us our debts as we also have forgiven our debtors.

Handle Criticism Wisely

IN AN 1862 CONVERSATION at the White House, Abraham Lincoln is reported to have said,

> "If I were to read, much less answer, all the attacks made on me, this shop might as well be closed for any other business. I do the very best I know — the very best I can; and I mean to keep doing so until the end. If the end brings me out all right, what is said against me won't amount to anything. If the end brings me out wrong, ten angels swearing I was right would make no difference."

Another former American President, Theodore Roosevelt adds,

> "The credit in life does not go to the critic who stands on the sideline and points out where the strong stumble, but rather, the real credit in life goes to the man who is actually in the arena, whose face may get marred by sweat and dust, who knows great enthusiasm and great devotion and learns to spend himself in a worthy cause, who, at best if he wins, knows the thrill of high achievement and if he fails, at least fails while daring greatly, so that in life his place will never be with those very cold and timid souls who know neither victory nor defeat."

Question:

Are you able to persist in the face of unjust criticism?

Excellence from 2 Timothy 4:5

> *But you, keep your head in all situations, endure hardship, do the work of an evangelist, discharge all the duties of your ministry.*

Humble Leadership

AFTER THE BATTLE OF GETTYSBURG, President Abraham Lincoln sensed an opportunity to end the war by driving hard against Lee's rear in retreat. As commander-in-chief, he ordered General Meade to attack swiftly. In a handwritten note along with the instructions for such an attack, Lincoln wrote:

> "The order I enclose is not of record. If you succeed, you need not publish the order. If you fail, publish it. Then, if you succeed, you will have all the credit of the movement. If not, I'll take all the responsibility."

That was the humble leadership of Abraham Lincoln. He was brave, self-effacing, and willing to let others take credit for successes. He was a true leader in word and deed.

Question:

Are you willing to let others take credit for the success you have had a part in achieving?

Excellence from Philippians 2:3

> *Do nothing out of selfish ambitions or vain conceit, but in humility, consider others better than yourselves.*

Judge Right From Wrong

While we can never judge a person's motives because we cannot see their heart, we must always judge behavior. In a day of sagging morals, Satan gives many excuses for illicit behavior. Pat McGee lists five situations where wrong is wrong, in spite of our excuses:

1. WRONG IS WRONG, even if we don't get caught.
   God sees all whether man does or not.
2. WRONG IS WRONG, even if done for a good cause.
   The end never justifies the means.
3. WRONG IS WRONG, even if others are doing worse things.
   God doesn't grade on a curve!
4. WRONG IS WRONG, even if it doesn't bother our conscience.
   The conscience can be educated to accept sin as normal, but it doesn't make sin right.
5. WRONG IS WRONG, even if it is commonly accepted.
   God doesn't establish morality by majority vote. What He says is wrong is wrong no matter who says other wise.

Question:

What evil is being called good today?

Excellence from 1 Thessalonians 5:21-22

> *Test everything. Hold on to the good. Avoid every kind of evil.*

Lead Your Children in Righteousness
Walk A Little Plainer, Daddy

"Walk a little plainer, Daddy,"
Said a little boy so frail,
"I'm following in your footsteps
And I don't want to fail.
Sometimes your steps are very plain;
Sometimes they're hard to see,
So walk a little plainer, Daddy
For you are leading me.

"I know that once you walked this way
Many years ago,
And what you did along the way
I'd really like to know;
For sometimes when I'm tempted
I don't know what to do,
So walk a little plainer, Daddy,
For I must follow you.

"Some day when I'm grown up
You are like I want to be,
Then I will have a little boy
Who will want to follow me.
And I would want to lead him right
And help him to be true . . .
So walk a little plainer, Daddy,
For we must follow you."

– Author Unknown

Question:
Are your steps distinctly righteous ones?

Excellence from Ephesians 6:4

Fathers, do not exasperate your children; instead, bring them up in the training and instruction of the Lord.

Leadership

Paradoxical Commandments of Leadership

1. People are illogical, unreasonable, and self-centered.
   Love them anyway.
2. If you do good, people will accuse you of selfish ulterior motives.
   Do good anyway.
3. If you are successful, you win false friends and true enemies.
   Succeed anyway.
4. The good you do today will be forgotten by tomorrow.
   Do good anyway.
5. Honesty and frankness make you vulnerable.
   Be honest and frank anyway.
6. The biggest men with the biggest ideas can be shot down by the smallest men with the smallest minds.
   Think big anyway.
7. People favor underdogs but follow only top dogs.
   Fight for a few underdogs anyway.
8. What you spend years building may be destroyed over night.
   Build anyway.
9. People really need help, but may attack you if you do help them.
   Help them anyway.
10. Give the world the best you have and you'll get kicked in the teeth.
    Give the world the best you have anyway.

– Author Unknown

Question:

How hard is it to faithfully do what you ought no matter who watches or approves?

Excellence from Philippians 2:14-15

Do everything without complaining or arguing, so that you may become blameless and pure, children of God without fault in a crooked and depraved generation, in which you shine like stars in the universe . . .

Learn to Live

FEW THINGS are so much at the mercy of life's fluctuations as money.

What can money do for you? It does not satisfy. The wealthier one becomes, the more money he wants.

Millionaires who laugh heartily are rare!

"What then are they doing if they are not laughing? They are carrying burdens which crush all laughter out of them. They are carrying the thing which promised to carry them" (J. H. Jowett).

In 1923, a very important meeting was held at the Edgewater Beach Hotel in Chicago. Attending this meeting were nine of the world's most successful financiers. Those present were:

the president of the largest independent steel company;
the president of the largest utility company;
the president of the largest gas company;
a great wheat speculator;
the president of the New York Stock Exchange;
a member of the President's Cabinet;
the greatest "bear" on Wall Street;
head of the world's greatest monopoly; and
the president of the bank of International Settlements.
These men had found the secret of making money.

TWENTY-FIVE YEARS LATER their situations had changed.

Charles Schwab lived on borrowed money and died bankrupt;
Samuel Insull died a fugitive from justice and penniless;
Howard Hopson was found insane;
Arthur Cutten died abroad insolvent;
Richard Whitney was released from prison;
Albert Fall was pardoned from prison so he could die at home;
Jesse Livermore died a suicide;
Ivar Krueger died a suicide; and
Leon Fraser died a suicide!

All these men learned well the art of making money, but not one of them had learned how to live.

Question:
Have you learned how to live or only how to make a living?

Excellence from Proverbs 11:28

Whoever trusts in his riches will fall, but the righteous will thrive like a green leaf.

Let God's Word Change Your Thinking

IN THE MID-1700s, JOHN NEWTON, the author of "Amazing Grace," was one of the most wicked men to sail the high seas in the awful business of slave-trading. He carried a rough leather whip at his belt, and many innocent Africans had their backs split open by its cruel lash. But one day, while reading a Bible in his cabin, John Newton accepted Jesus Christ as his Savior. He repented immediately for his involvement in the slave trade, and he later helped get legislation passed by the British Parliament to outlaw this deplorable practice in the commonwealth. He had this inscription written on his tombstone: "I, John Newton, once an infidel, once a libertine, a servant of slaves, was by the rich mercy of our Lord Jesus Christ preserved, pardoned, restored, and called to proclaim the faith I had long labored to destroy."

Question:

What effect does God's Word have on your beliefs and actions?

Excellence from Psalm 119:11

I have hidden your word in my heart that I might not sin against you.

Live A Transparent Life

You don't have to tell how you live each day,
You don't have to say if you work or play,
A tried, true barometer serves in the place—
However you live, it will show in your face.

The false, the deceit that you bear in your heart,
Will not stay inside where it first gets its start;
For sinew and blood are thin veils of lace—
What you wear on your heart, you wear in your face.

If you've gambled and won in the great game of life;
If you feel you have conquered the sorrow and strife,
If you've played the game fair and you stand on first base,
You don't have to say so; it shows in your face.

If your life is unselfish, and for others you live,
For not what you get, but how much you give;
If you live close to God in His infinite grace—
You don't have to tell it; it shows in your face.

– Author Unknown

Question:

Do you realize that both good and evil cannot remain hidden?

Excellence from Proverbs 5:13

A happy heart makes the face cheerful . . .

Live One Day At A Time

THE LORD GRACIOUSLY BLESSED US with a precious son. He was paralyzed and able to sit in his wheelchair only with the assistance of full-length body braces. One of the nation's most respected gynecologists and obstetricians brought him into the world. Tragically, this man—overcome by grief—sought to find the answer in a bourbon bottle rather than in a blessed Bible. Due to the doctor's intoxication at the time of delivery, he inexcusably bungled his responsibility. Several of the baby's bones were broken. His leg was pulled out at the growing center. Needless abuse—resulting in hemorrhaging of the brain — was inflicted upon the little fellow. (Let me pause long enough to say that this is no indictment upon doctors. I thank God for doctors. This man was a tragic exception. He was banned from practice in some hospitals, and, as mentioned previously, he committed suicide.)

During the first year of the little lad's life, eight doctors said he could not possibly survive. For the first two years of his life my wife had to feed him every three hours with a Brecht feeder. It took a half hour to prepare for the feeding and it took another half hour to clean up and put him back to bed. Not once during that time did she ever get out of the house for any diversion whatsoever. Never did she get more than two hours sleep at one time.

My wife, formerly Christine Barker of Bristol, Virginia, had once been acclaimed by some of the nation's leading musicians as one of the outstanding contemporary female vocalists in America. From the time she was thirteen she had been popular as a singer — and constantly in the public eye. Hers was the experience of receiving and rejecting some fancy offers with even fancier incomes to marry an aspiring Baptist pastor with no church to pastor!

Then, after five years of marriage, tragedy struck! The whole episode was so unnecessary. Eight of the nation's leading doctors said that our son would not survive. From a life of public service she was now marooned within the walls of our home. Her beautiful voice no longer enraptured public audiences with the story of Jesus, but was not silenced, or at best, muted to the subdued humming of lullabies.

Had it not been from her spiritual maturity whereby she laid hold of the resources of God and lived one day at a time, this heart-rending experience would long since have caused an emotional breakdown.

John Edmund, Jr., our little son, lived more than twenty years. We rejoice that he committed his heart and life to Jesus Christ and gave evidence of a genuine concern for the things of the Lord. I attribute his commitment to Jesus Christ and his wonderful disposition to the sparkling radiance of an emotionally mature, Christ-centered mother who has mastered the discipline of living one day at a time. Never have I — nor has anyone else — heard a word of complaint from her. The people who know her concur that at thirty-five years of age and after having been subjected to more grief than many people twice her age, she possessed sparkle that would be the envy of any high school senior and the radiance and charm for which any debutante would gladly give a fortune.

Seize today. Live for today. Wring it dry of every opportunity.

– John Edmund Haggai

Question:

What trial do you face that can only be met one day at a time?

Excellence from Matthew 6:34

Therefore, do not worry about tomorrow, for tomorrow will worry about itself. Each day has enough trouble of its own.

Live With Class

What is Class?

CLASS NEVER RUNS SCARED. It is sure-footed and confident in the knowledge that you can meet life head-on and handle whatever comes along.

Jacob had it. Esau didn't. Symbolically, we can look to Jacob's wrestling match with the angel. Those who have class have wrestled with their own personal "angel" and won a victory that marks them thereafter.

Class never makes excuses. It takes its lumps and learns from past mistakes.

Class is considerate of others. It knows that good manners are nothing more than a series of petty sacrifices.

Class bespeaks an aristocracy that has nothing to do with ancestors or money. The most affluent blue blood can be totally without class while the descendant of a Welsh miner may ooze class from every pore.

Class never tries to build itself up by tearing others down.

Class is already up and need not strive to look better by making others look worse.

Class can "walk with kings and keep its virtue, and talk with crowds and keep the common touch." Everyone is comfortable with the person who has class — because he is comfortable with himself.

If you have class, you don't need much of anything else. If you don't have it, no matter what else you have — it doesn't make much difference.

– Author Unknown

Question:

Who do you know who lives with extreme class?

Excellence from Colossians 3:17

And whatever you do, whether in word or deed, do it all in the name of the Lord Jesus, giving thanks to God the Father through him.

Love Handicapped People

BACK DURING THE SECOND WORLD WAR, the parents of a sailor from New Jersey went for several weeks without hearing anything from their son. Finally, they gave up and considered him a war victim. Near the end of the war, the parents received a phone call from someone in San Diego, California. After a moment on the phone, the parents recognized the voice as that of their son. He was alive!

During the course of the conversation the son explained to his parents that for the past several months he had found it difficult to write because he had been taking care of a war victim. He told them that the person had been wounded in the war and had lost a leg, an arm, an eye, and part of his face.

His parents expressed concern over the poor sailor and then bragged on their son for taking care of him during all those months. The boy then asked his parents for permission to bring the injured boy home to live with them. He explained that the boy didn't have another home, nor anyone to care for him. His parents expressed their concern for the wounded sailor and told their son that they thought it was very noble of him to want to bring the sailor home with him. But after some conversation, the parents expressed their desire to their son that he not bring the boy home with him. They simply didn't want the job of taking care of such a battle-scarred sailor. Their son said he understood their feelings and said that he would not bring the boy home. Expressing his love for the parents, the sailor son hung up.

You know, I guess it is hard to fulfill such a request as the sailor son made. Most of us don't want a disfigured person around the house, do we? None of us like to look at ugly things, and most of us judge a person's beauty by his physical appearance. We appreciate the good that handicapped people have done. But we would just rather not have to be burdened with them around the house.

Many times we feel sorry for the physically handicapped. So we give them a little something that requires no effort on our part and does them little good. But the handicapped person wants more than anything else to be treated like a human being.

The morning after they spoke with their son, the couple in New Jersey received a telegram from the Naval officials stating that their son had jumped from a window to his death. The parents couldn't understand why their son had reacted so to their request until the body arrived and the casket was opened. Their son had only one arm, one leg, one eye, and a badly disfigured face.

Maybe we should try a little harder to love those who simply want to be treated like a human being.

– Author Unknown

Question:

Do you show love to the handicapped or do you shun them?

Excellence from Matthew 25:40

> The king will reply, "I tell you the truth, whatever you did for one of the least of these brothers of mine, you did for me."

Excellence Illustrated

Maintain A Healthy Mind-Set

THE DAMAGE A MIND-SET CAN DO is dramatically illustrated by the
sinking of the *Titanic* on her maiden voyage in 1912, with the
loss of 1,513 lives. Designed to be the safest ship afloat, the
Titanic was equipped with a double bottom and sixteen watertight compartments. A mind-set that she was unsinkable
seems to have been largely responsible for the disaster.

She carried lifeboats sufficient for only one-third of her
capacity, and no assignment of passengers was made to these
boats; nor were any drills held. The *Titanic* was unsinkable.

Three days out of Queenstown, she received her first
wireless warning of icebergs in the steamer lanes. A few hours
later she received another message about icebergs, but the
wireless operator was too busy with his accounts to bother
recording the message. The *Titanic* was unsinkable.

That afternoon another warning was received. This time
the operator sent it to the Captain, who glanced at it casually
and handed it without comment to the managing director of
the White Star Line. By 9:30 that night at least five warnings
of icebergs had been received, and the *Titanic* was nearing
their reported location. But no precautions were taken other
than to warn the lookouts to be alert. The owners wanted a
speed record; the *Titanic* steamed ahead into the darkness at
twenty-two knots. The *Titanic* was unsinkable.

She had yet another chance. At 11:30 p.m. the wireless
crackled with a message from the *Californian:* "Say, old man,
we are stuck here, surrounded by ice." But the mind-set held,
and the *Titanic's* operator replied, "Shut up, shut up, keep
out. I am talking to Cape Race; you are jamming my signals."
The *Titanic* steamed ahead at twenty-two knots; she was
unsinkable.

Ten minutes later the lookout spotted a giant iceberg dead
ahead. Officers on the bridge did what they could to avoid the
crash, but it was too late. The collision ripped a hundred-yard
gash in the ship's double bottom. Although the watertight
doors were closed immediately, the bulkheads not already
damaged gave way, one by one. The great ship was doomed.

The loading of the lifeboats went slowly and badly, in part
because the passengers would not believe that so safe a ship

45

could sink. The boats left the ship with nearly five hundred passengers less than capacity. At best there would have been room for no more than a thousand. Even so the casualties might have been few. Distress calls were sent out within minutes after the collision, and the ship did not sink until more than two hours later. A number of ships raced to the scene, in spite of the ice. But they were too far away to save the fifteen hundred who did not get into the lifeboats. Meantime, the *Californian* was lying within sight of the *Titanic*, possibly no more than five miles away. Her radio operator did not hear the *Titanic's* wireless calls; he had gone to bed shortly after being told to "shut up." Some of her crew did see the *Titanic's* lights and rocket signals but did nothing more than try to communicate with the unknown ship by blinker. Testimony in the investigation of the disaster showed that the sea was calm and the night clear, and that the *Californian* might easily have pushed through the ice field to rescue most if not all of the passengers. Perhaps her officers, too, had a mind-set.

– W. Edgar Moore

Question:
What mind-set do you have that ought to be changed.

Excellence from Romans 8:6

The mind of sinful man is death, but the mind controlled by the Spirit is life and peace.

Excellence Illustrated

Make A Difference

AS AN ELDERLY GENTLEMAN walked the beach at dawn, he noticed a young man ahead of him picking up starfish and flinging them into the sea. Finally catching up with the youth, he asked him why he was doing this. The answer was that the stranded starfish would die if left until the morning sun. "But the beach goes on for miles and there are millions of starfish," countered the elderly man. "How can your effort make any difference?" The young man looked at the starfish in his hand and then threw it to the safety of the waves. "It makes a difference to this one," he said.

Question:

Will you purpose in your heart to make a difference to someone today?

Excellence from Titus 3:8

> . . those who have trusted in God may (should) be careful to devote themselves to doing what is good.

Excellence Illustrated

Master Your Emotions

THERE WAS ONCE A TIGER KEEPER and a tiger cub who lived together. The keeper wanted the tiger for a pet, a friend. He fed
him, walked him, cared for him. He always spoke softly,
warmly to him. But as the tiger grew, his green eyes began to
glow with hostility. His muscles rippled their warning of
power. One night, when the keeper was off guard, a lovely girl
happened by. The claws reached out. There was a scream.
The keeper arrived too late. Then others felt the tiger's teeth —
a boy, a man. And the keeper in panic prayed that the tiger
might die, but still he lived. In fear, the keeper caged him in a
deep, dark hole where no one could get near. Now the tiger
roared night and day. The keeper could not work or sleep
through the roars of his guilt. Then he prayed that God might
tame the tiger. God answered, "Let the tiger out of the cave. I
will give you strength to face him." The keeper, willing to die,
opened the door. The tiger came out. They stood. Stared.
When the tiger saw no fear in the keeper's eyes, he lay down
at his feet. Life with the tiger began. At night he would roar,
but the keeper would look him straight in the eye, face him
again and again. The tiger was never completely in his power,
although as years passed they became friends. The keeper
could touch him. But he never took his eyes off him, or off
God who gave him the strength to tame the beast. Only then
was he free from the roar of remorse, the growl of guilt, the
raging of his own evil.

– Augsberger
Seventy Times Seven

You are the keeper. The tiger is a part of you that would
destroy you if given its own way. It could be regret of the past,
remorse for past choices, guilt over forgiven sin, emotions of
lust, fear or unfulfilled desires. Only God can give you the
strength to rule over the tiger inside before it masters you! He
will set you free from the tyranny of the tiger. Then, he sup-
plies strength to live in freedom so that the true you, made in
God's image, begins to live again!

Question:
What "tiger" do you need to have God's help to hold in check?

Excellence from Galatians 5:24

Those who belong to Christ Jesus have crucified the sinful nature with its passions and desires.

Meet Jesus Every Day
I Met the Master

I had walked life's way with an easy tread,
Had followed where comforts and pleasures led,
Until one day in a quiet place
I met the Master face to face.

With station and rank and wealth for my goal,
Much thought for my body but none for my soul,
I had entered to win in life's mad race,
When I met the Master face to face.

I met Him and knew Him and blushed to see,
That His eyes full of sorrow were fixed on me;
And I faltered and fell at His feet that day,
While my castles melted and vanished away.

Melted and vanished and in their place
Naught else did I see but the Master's face.
And I cried aloud, "Oh, make me meet
to follow the steps of Thy wounded feet."

My thought is now for souls of men,
I have lost my life to find it again,
E'er since one day in a quiet place
I met the Master face to face.

– Anonymous

Question:
Do you meet with your Master every day?

Excellence from Revelation 3:20

Here I am! I stand at the door and knock. If anyone hears my voice and opens the door, I will come in and eat with him and he with me.

Excellence Illustrated

Meet Needs of Others

WHEN CONSTANTINOPLE WAS BESIEGED by the Turks in the fifteenth century, and the Christian garrison was hard-pressed, they sent for the priests and monks, that they might go up and down the lines encouraging the troops and imparting spiritual reassurance. But the churchmen sent back word that it would . . . "interrupt their periods of formal worship and devotion;" therefore, they begged to be excused. And on the same ground, many of Christ's followers have excused themselves from practical participation in spiritual conflicts which would have advanced the rule of God in the lives of men.

– L. H. Bugbee

Question:
Who has a need that you can meet?

Excellence from Philippians 2:4

Each of you should look not only to your own interests, but also to the interests of others.

51

Excellence Illustrated

Obedience

LEGEND HAS IT THAT A LONG TIME AGO, Mohammed decided he would breed a strain of horses that would be the best to be found anywhere in the world. He gathered together the finest horsemen and sent them on a mission to bring back the finest stallions to be found. No cost was too great, no region too remote for them to search out the world's finest horses.

One by one, the horsemen returned with some great stallions. They came from all regions, climates, colors and breeding backgrounds. The final count was 100 stallions.

Mohammed took over the training of these magnificent animals. He trained them daily. He would blow a bugle; and when he did, the horses would run at full speed, stopping right at the feet of their master. Mohammed did this again and again.

After one year of this special training, Mohammed felt it was time for the final test. This test came after a four-day period in which these 100 horses were penned up in a corral with neither food nor water. The Middle East is a very hot land, and the horses became extremely thirsty.

In the late afternoon of the fourth day Mohammed applied his ultimate test. He opened the gates to the corral where the horses had been enclosed. Two hundred yards away was a cool stream in a valley where they were accustomed to drinking during their year of training.

The thirsty animals ran at full gallop toward the cool stream to quench their thirst. Just as they arrived at the stream, Mohammed blew his bugle and called them all back up the hill to stand in front of him. Out of the hundred wonderful animals, only one turned when he heard the bugle and raced back at full speed to stand in front of his master.

Tradition has it that from the loins of this great horse arose the famous Arabian breed of horses. They have been accorded the compliment of being the finest strain of horses ever bred. They have produced thousands of champions in all areas of competition. They are indeed a great breed of horseflesh.

Dwight L. Moody said once, "Give me one totally committed man for God, and I'll win a city for Christ!"

We often think just one person cannot do much. Yet, from one stallion came a great breed of horses. And God can use just one committed, disciplined and willing servant.

– Dan Stavely

Question:
Do you obey the commands of God no matter how thirsty your flesh?

Excellence from Romans 6:17

You have been set free from sin and have become slaves to righteousness.

Excellence Illustrated

Obey Your Real Boss

Think of yourself as living in an apartment house. You live
there under a landlord who has made your life miserable. He
charges you exorbitant rent. When you can't pay, he loans
you money at a fearful rate of interest, to get you even further
into his debt. He barges into your apartment at all hours of
the day and night, wrecks and dirties the place up, then
charges you extra for not maintaining the premises. Your life
is miserable.

Then comes Someone who says, "I've taken over this
apartment house. I've purchased it. You can live here as long
as you like, free. The rent is paid up. I am going to be living
here with you, in the manager's apartment."

What a joy! You are saved! You are delivered out of the
clutches of the old landlord!

But what happens? You hardly have time to rejoice in your
new-found freedom, when a knock comes at the door. And
there he is — the old landlord! Mean, glowering, and demand-
ing as ever. He has come for the rent, he says.

What do you do? Do you pay him? Of course, you don't.
Do you go out and pop him on the nose? No — he's bigger
than you are.

You confidently tell him, "You'll have to take that up with
the new Landlord." He may bellow, threaten, wheedle, and
cajole. You just quietly tell him, "Take it up with the new
Landlord." If he comes back a dozen times, with all sorts of
threats and arguments, waving legal-looking documents in
your face, you simply tell him yet once again, "Take it up with
the new Landlord." In the end he has to. He knows it, too. He
just hopes that he can bluff and threaten and deceive you into
doubting that the new landlord will really take care of things.

Now this is the situation of a Christian. Once Christ has
delivered you from the power of sin and the devil, you can
depend on it: that old landlord will soon come back knocking
at your door. And what is your defense? How do you keep him
from getting the whip hand over you again? You send him to
the new Landlord. You send him to Jesus.

– Larry Christenson

Question:

For what forgiven sin, bad decision, or regret does Satan try to keep making you pay?

Excellence from 1 Peter 5:8, 9

Be self-controlled and alert. Your enemy the devil prowls around like a roaring lion looking for someone to devour. Resist him, standing firm in the faith . . .

Overcome Discouragement

THE TEMPTATION to be discouraged is common to everyone.

Walt Disney was dismissed from a major newspaper and he was told he had no talent as an artist; explorer Richard Byrd crash-landed the first two times he soloed in a plane and the third time he flew head-on into another plane; writer Rod Serling wrote and marketed 40 stores before he sold one; western writer Zane Grey was fired by five papers because he couldn't do the job as a reporter.

Certainly, these men were tempted to be discouraged and give up in their careers. But they persisted and the future was brighter than the past!

Things may not be the best at present. But circumstances change quickly. Events occur which can make things better almost overnight. The future can be brighter than the past.

Calvin Coolidge once said, "Nothing in the world can take the place of persistence. Talent will not; nothing is more common than unsuccessful men with talent. Genius will not; unrewarded genius is almost a proverb. Education will not; the world is full of educated derelicts. Persistence and determination alone are omnipotent."

Years ago, boxer Jim Corbett was asked why he was able to win the championship. "Because I fought one more round," he said.

Question:

What would it take for you to "fight one more round?"

Excellence from Hebrews 12:7

Endure hardship as discipline; God is treating you as sons.

Own Your Faults

"WE OFTEN THINK that we have no need of anyone else's advice or reproof. Always remember, much grace does not imply much enlightenment. We may be wise but have little love, or we may have love with little wisdom. God has wisely joined us all together as the parts of a body so that we cannot say to another, I have no need of you.

Even to imagine that those who are not saved cannot teach you is a very great and serious mistake. Dominion is not found in Grace. Not observing this has led some into many mistakes and certainly into pride. Beware even the appearance of pride! Let there be in you that lowly mind which was in Christ Jesus. Be clothed with humility. Let modesty appear in all your words and actions.

One way we do this is to own any fault we have. If you have at any time thought, spoken or acted wrong, do not refrain from acknowledging it. Never dream that this will hurt the cause of God. In fact, it will further it. Be open and honest when you are rebuked and do not seek to evade it or disguise it. Rather, let it appear just as it is and you will thereby not hinder, but adorn the gospel."

– John Wesley

Question:

What shortcomings must you acknowledge and work to improve?

Excellence from James 5:16

> *Therefore confess your sins to each other and pray for each other so that you may be healed.*

Pay the Price for Success

LIFE IS NEVER EASY. Anyone who would achieve will have to struggle against adversity. He must develop character, and character is developed through suffering. We must pay the *price* of success or the *cost* of failure! Sometimes it seems we pay the price several times before becoming and achieving what God wants us to be and to do.

Our faith says that God knows what He is doing. The following lines are penned to strengthen that faith:

God Knows What He's About

When God wants to drill a man,
And thrill a man, and skill a man;
When God wants to mold a man
To play the noblest part;
When He yearns with all His heart
To create so great and bold a man
That all the world shall be amazed,
Watch His methods, watch His ways
How He ruthlessly perfects
Whom He royally elects!
How He hammers him or hurts him
And with mighty blows converts him
Into trial shapes of clay which
Only God can understand.

– Anonymous

Question:

Is your faith in God strong enough to persist in becoming and doing what you can become and do?

Excellence from Romans 5:3-5

We rejoice in our sufferings, because we know that suffering produces perseverance; perseverance character; and character, hope. And hope does not disappoint us, because God has poured out his love into our hearts by the Holy Spirit whom he has given us.

58

Perform the Essential
Above the Immediate

A LIGHTHOUSE ALONG A RUGGED COAST was tended by a keeper who was given enough oil for one month at a time and told to keep the light burning every night. One day a woman asked for oil so that her children could stay warm. Then a farmer came. His son needed oil for a lamp so he could read. Someone else needed oil for an engine. The keeper saw each as a worthy request and measured out enough oil to satisfy all. Near the end of the month, the tank in the lighthouse ran dry. That night the beacon was dark and three ships crashed on the rocks. More than 100 lives were lost. When a government official investigated, the keeper explained what he had done and why. "You were given one task alone," insisted the official. "It was to keep the light burning. Everything else was secondary. There is no defense."

Question:
What essential task are you given that you must not neglect?

Excellence from Galatians 5:7

You were running a good race. Who cut in on you and kept you from obeying the truth?

Persistence I

IN THE FIRST HALF OF THE EIGHTEENTH CENTURY, there was a young boy who aspired to be a writer. Because of his lack of formal education, the boy wasn't sure of his ability. And his life had not been one that would foster self-confidence. His family had moved quite often, his father finally being jailed because of his inability to pay his debts. Because of the circumstances, this young boy had been able to attend school for only four years.

To earn a living he got a job putting labels on bottles of blacking in a dilapidated warehouse. He found a dismal attic in which to sleep, and he shared that room with others who couldn't afford anything better.

This young boy was determined to write. He wrote day after day. Finally he got enough courage to submit a manuscript to a publisher. He mailed that manuscript at night, when no one could see him, because he was afraid someone might ridicule him. Soon he heard from the publisher. His manuscript was refused.

Time and again he submitted his writings. Again and again the same answer came back — rejected! No publisher or paper was interested in his writings. But the desire to write was burning in the young boy's heart and he refused to quit.

Finally, one of his stores was accepted. He didn't receive any money for the story, but the editor did give him some praise. It was such a happy moment for him that he walked the streets with tears of joy coming down his cheeks. Now someone else had shown some belief in him.

This bit of encouragement gave that young boy the impetus he needed to go on to greater things. And in a few years all of England was reading his writings. The young boy believed in himself and believed he was capable of reaching the dream he had in his heart. For that reason, he would not quit.

Too often in life we quit too soon. Many times the victory is just around the corner if we would only keep trying.

It is of great importance that a person believe in himself. *Selling ourselves short is no virtue.* It is a vice. It hurts us. It keeps us from developing our God-given resources to become all that we can become — all that God wants us to become.

In the sovereignty of God, our dreams can come true. But we must remember that the fulfillment of any dream requires dedication, sacrifice, and persistence on our part.

The young boy in London who refused to quit was Charles Dickens. His novels are still read to this day. He believed in himself and his God-given talent to write. And he persisted until his dream came true!

Question:

For what dream should you persist?

Excellence from Matthew 7:7-8

Ask and it will be given to you; seek and you will find; knock and the door will be opened to you. For everyone who asks receives; he who seeks finds; and to him who knocks, the door will be opened.

Persistence II

IT'S A RARE INDIVIDUAL who does not get discouraged. Regardless of who it happens to, the key to overcoming discouragement and temporary failure is persistence and perseverance.

The value of persistence, perseverance and courage has rarely been illustrated more convincingly than in the life of this man — a great individual who persisted until he finally reached success.

But he suffered many defeats along the way. This man . . .

> . . . failed in business at age 22;
> . . . ran for the Legislature and lost at age 23;
> . . . once again failed in business at age 24;
> . . . was finally elected to the Legislature at age 25;
> . . . lost his sweetheart at age 26;
> . . . suffered a nervous breakdown at age 27;
> . . . was defeated in the race for Speaker at age 29;
> . . . was defeated in the race for Elector at age 31;
> . . . lost the Congressional race at age 34;
> . . . was finally elected to Congress at age 37;
> . . . lost his Congressional seat at age 39;
> . . . was defeated in the Senatorial race for the Vice-Presidency at age 47;
> . . . was once again defeated in the Senatorial race at age 49;
> . . . but was elected to the Presidency of the United States at age 51.

This is the record of Abraham Lincoln. He is the one who said, "Things may come to those who wait, but only things left by those who hustle."

Question:

Through what discouragement must you persist?

Excellence from Philippians 3:14

> *I press on toward the goal to win the prize for which God has called me heavenward in Christ Jesus.*

Pray with People in Need

JOHN DILLINGER, declared "public enemy number one" by the FBI, was the most ruthless and notorious gangster of the 1930s. As a teenager, Dillinger attended Sunday School. A documented article relates the story:

> In a little country church in Indiana there are some Sunday School records that have John Dillinger's name on them. Young John Dillinger went to Sunday School for seven Sundays, then he missed. Then he went, then he missed and missed. Finally, by the name of John Dillinger is written: "Dropped."

Why was Dillinger a Sunday School dropout? An article from Rex Humbard's *Answer* magazine provides the surprising answer:

> Back in 1942 we were in Cadle Tabernacle at Indianapolis. A lady came up to me after I had prayed with many young people that night. We had over 8,000 there and when I gave the invitation many hundreds came forward for prayer.
> As I was getting ready to leave this nice looking lady took me by the hand and said, "Rex, you don't know me, but I want to thank you for praying with those young people. Years ago my brother got into trouble in our community. People there told their children, "Don't have anything to do with John, because he's a bad boy." We had a meeting in a country church and one night during that meeting John's heart was moved. He got up out of his seat and came down to the altar. But because no one came to pray with him, in just a few moments John got up and walked to the back of the church. He looked at me and said, "I'm never going into another church again." He didn't. My brother's name was John Dillinger."
> Tears welled up in that woman's eyes as she told me her story. I remembered reading about Dillinger. He had used the powers of his life to glorify evil. Years

63

ago his heart was tender, but he turned from God that night.

Certainly Dillinger was morally responsible for his actions, but the fact that no one counseled with him after he responded to a public invitation must be considered a contributing factor. According to his own testimony, it was this oversight that turned him away from God.

Question:
Is there someone you should be praying with instead of shunning?

Excellence from Matthew 18:12

If a man owns a hundred sheep, and one of them wanders away, will he not leave the ninety-nine on the hills and go to look for the one that wandered off?

Refuse to Gossip

Forget It

If you see a tall fellow ahead of the crowd,
A leader of men, marching fearless and proud,
And you know of a tale whose mere telling aloud
Would cause this proud head to in anguish be bowed,
It's a pretty good plan to forget it.

If you know of a skeleton hidden away
In a closet, and guarded and kept from the day
In the dark, whose showing, whose sudden display
Would cause grief and sorrow and life-long dismay —
It's a pretty good plan to forget it.

If you know of a spot in the life of a friend,
(We all have such spots concealed, world without end.)
Whose touching his heart strings would play on and rend
Till the shame of its showing no grieving could mend,
It's a pretty good plan to forget it.

If you know anything that will darken the joy
Of a man or a woman, a girl or a boy,
That will wipe out a smile or the least way annoy
A fellow, or cause any gladness to cloy,
It's a pretty good plan to forget it.

– Anonymous

Question:

Will you agree with your tongue to only speak things that help build others up?

Excellence from James 4:11

> *Brothers, do not slander one another . . .*

Remain Humble

Humility

I asked God for strength,
    that I might achieve.
I was made weak,
    that I might learn humbly to obey.

I asked for help,
    that I might do greater things.
I was given infirmity,
    that I might do better things.

I asked for riches,
    that I might be happy.
I was given poverty,
    that I might be wise.

I asked for all things,
    that I might enjoy life.
I was given life,
    that I might enjoy all things.

I got nothing that I asked for,
    but everything I had hoped for.
Despite myself, my prayers were answered.
    I am among all men, most richly blessed.
        – An Anonymous Soldier of the Confederacy

Question:
Can you humbly thank God in all things?

Excellence from 1 Thessalonians 5:16-18

Be joyful always; pray continually; give thanks in all circumstances, for this is God's will for you in Christ Jesus.

Return Good for Evil

EDWIN M. STANTON LIVED FROM 1814 TO 1869. He was a nervous, asthmatic, cranky, and contradictory lawyer who worked his way up after dropping out of college because of lack of funds. Stanton served as the Attorney General in the Cabinet of President James Buchanan.

Stanton was also a sharp critic of Abraham Lincoln, and had many unkind words for the man who followed Buchanan as President of the United States. He often spoke of Lincoln as "a low cunning clown" and even nicknamed him "the original gorilla." Stanton went so far as to suggest to a famous hunter of the time that he was a fool to wander over to Africa trying to catch a gorilla when he could have easily found one in Springfield, Illinois.

After Lincoln was elected President, he was influential in acquiring a post as legal adviser to Simon Cameron, Secretary of War, for Stanton. Even after this favor, Stanton continued his harsh criticism of Lincoln.

Many people were shocked when Lincoln appointed Stanton as the Secretary of War following the resignation of Cameron. It was hard for them to understand why Lincoln would give such a high, important post to a man who had continually criticized him and his policy.

While Stanton was treating Lincoln in such a manner, Lincoln continued to show Stanton every courtesy. He never spoke to him harshly, or returned hateful remarks with hateful remarks. Lincoln appointed Stanton to the job of Secretary of War for one simple reason — Stanton was the best man for the job. Lincoln knew this, and did not let the ugliness of Stanton stop him from making the appointment.

On the night of April 14, 1865, Lincoln was watching a play entitled "Our American Cousin" from a box at Ford's theater in Washington. During the play a man named John Wilkes Booth entered the box where Lincoln was sitting and shot the President in the head. During the confusion that followed Lincoln was carried to a little room where an attempt was made to save his life.

Into that room that night came several people. They watched — stunned — as their President lay dying. Among those who were there was Edwin Stanton, the man who had been so harsh and critical of the President, despite the fact that the President had shown him every courtesy and kindness. Looking down at the rugged form of a gentle man, Stanton spoke through the tears: "There lies the greatest ruler of men the world has ever seen."

A Galilean Carpenter once said: "Love your enemies and pray for your persecutors and those who treat you spitefully." Stanton learned the hard way that this was the highest and noblest way of living ever given mankind. His criticism was finally silenced — by love.

– Don Wildmon

Question:

To whom do you have the opportunity to return good for evil?

Excellence from Luke 6:27

But I tell you who hear me: Love your enemies, do good to those who hate you; bless those who curse you, pray for those who mistreat you.

Seek Truth Over Tradition

FOR CENTURIES, PEOPLE BELIEVED that Aristotle was right when he said that the heavier an object, the faster it would fall to earth. Aristotle was regarded as the greatest thinker of all times and surely he could not be wrong. All it would have taken was for one brave person to take two objects, one heavy and one light, and drop them from a great height to see whether or not the heavier object landed first. But no one stepped forward until nearly 2000 years after Aristotle's death. In 1589, Galileo summoned learned professors to the base of the leaning Tower of Pisa. Then he went to the top and pushed off a ten-pound and a one-pound weight. Both landed at the same time. But the power of belief in the conventional wisdom was so strong that the professors denied what they had seen. They continued to say Aristotle was right.

– Executive Speechwriter Newsletter

Question:

Do you seek truth or merely accept what your tradition says is truth?

Excellence from John 14:6

Jesus answered, "I am the way and the truth and the life. No one comes to the Father except through me."

Stay Away from Sin

A CERTAIN KIND OF EAGLE attacks seals as they swim in the water. The bird circles, swoops down, and fixes its claws into the flesh of its prey. Then it pulls the victim ashore and kills it. Sometimes, however, the eagle picks on a seal too strong to handle. With a mighty lunge, the seal heads for deep water drowning the helplessly attached bird with it. Despite the eagle's shriek of horror and flapping of wings, its talons remain fixed and it is drowned.

Sin is too big for man to handle in his own strength. It always takes us further than we want to go, makes us stay longer than we want to stay, and makes us pay more than we want to pay. When faced with a fork in the road of life, God allows us to choose which way to go. But we can never choose where that road takes us! Stay away from the highway of sin!

Question:

What fork in your road must you choose to stay away from sin?

Excellence from 2 Timothy 2:22

Flee the evil desires of youth and pursue righteousness, faith, love, and peace . . .

Stay Near Great People

THERE ARE MANY PEOPLE who could be Olympic Champions, All-Americans who have never tried. I'd estimate five million people could have beaten me in the pole vault the years I won it, at least five million. Men that were stronger, bigger and faster than I was could have done it, but they never picked up a pole, never made the feeble effort to pick their legs off the ground trying to get over the bar.

Greatness is all around us! It's easy to be great because great people will help you. What is fantastic about all the conventions I go to is that the greatest in the business will come and share their ideas, their methods and their techniques with everyone else. I have seen the greatest salesmen open up and show young salesmen exactly how they did it. They don't hold back. I have also found it true in the world of sports.

I'll never forget the time I was trying to break Dutch Warmerdam's record. I was about a foot below his record, so I called him on the phone. I said, "Dutch, can you help me? I've seemed to level off; I can't get any higher." He said, "Sure, Bob, come on up to visit me and I'll give you all I got." I spent three days with the master, the greatest pole vaulter in the world. For three days, Dutch gave me everything that he'd seen. There were things that I was doing wrong and he corrected them. To make a long story short, I went up eight inches. That great guy gave me the best that he had. I've found that sports champions and heroes willingly do this just to help you become great.

John Wooden has a philosophy that every day he is supposed to help someone who can never reciprocate; that's his obligation.

When in college working on his Masters' Thesis on scouting and defensive football, George Allen wrote up a 30-page survey and sent it out to the great coaches in the country. Eighty-five percent answered it completely.

Great people will share, and that is what made George Allen one of the greatest football coaches in the world. Great people will tell you their secrets. Look for them, call them on the phone or buy their books. Go where they are, get around

71

them, talk to them. It is easy to be great when you get around great people.

– Bob Richards - Pole Vaulter
—Two Time Olympic Gold Medalist

Question:

Are you around people who lift you up or tear you down?

Excellence from Mark 10:43-44

Whoever wants to become great among you must be your servant, and whoever wants to be first must be slaves of all.

Stop Compromising

YEARS AGO, FOOTBALL GREAT BUBBA SMITH gave up a very lucrative, amusing, and easy job making beer commercials because he realized it was wrong. Here, in his own words is how it happened.

"I went back to Michigan State for the homecoming parade last year," Bubba said. "I was the grand marshal and I was riding in the back seat of this car. The people were yelling, but they weren't saying, 'Go, State, go.' One side of the street was yelling, 'Tastes great' and the other side was yelling 'Less filling.'

"Then we go to the stadium. The older folks are yelling, 'Kill, Bubba, kill!' But the students are yelling 'Tastes great! Less filling!' Everyone in the stands is drunk. It was like I was contributing to alcohol, and I don't drink. It made me realize I was doing something I didn't want to do.

"I was with my brother, Tody, who is my agent. I told him, 'Tody, I'll never do another Lite beer commercial.'

"I loved doing the commercials, but I didn't like the effect it was having on a lot of little people. I'm talking about people in school. Kids would come up to me on the street and recite lines from my commercials, verbatim. They knew the lines better than I did. It was scary. Kids start to listen to things you say, you want to tell 'em something that is the truth.

"Doing those commercials, it's like me telling everyone in school, 'Hey, it's cool to have a Lite beer.' I'd go to places like Daytona Beach and Fort Lauderdale on spring breaks [as a spokesman for the brewery], and it was scary to see how drunk those kids were. It was fun talking to the fans, until you see people lying on the beach because they can't make it back to their rooms, or tearing up a city.

"As the years wear on, you stop compromising your principles."

Question:

What principles are you compromising?

Excellence from Ephesians 5:15-16

Be very careful, then, how you live — not as unwise but as wise, making the most of every opportunity, because the days are evil.

Strive for Perfection

IF 99.9 PERCENT IS GOOD ENOUGH, then it's also okay that .. .

- Two million documents will be lost by the IRS this year.
- 811,000 faulty rolls of 35mm film will be loaded this year.
- 22,999 checks will be deducted from the wrong bank accounts in the next 60 minutes.
- 2,488,200 books will be shipped in the next twelve months with the wrong covers.
- 5,517,200 cases of soft drinks produced in the next twelve months will be flatter than a bad tire.
- 18,322 pieces of mail will be mishandled in the next hour.
- 880,000 credit cards in circulation will turn out to have incorrect cardholder information on their magnetic strips.
- 114,500 mismatched pairs of shoes will be shipped this year.
- 315 entries in *Webster's Third New International Dictionary of the English Language* will turn out to be misspelled.

– *The Working Communicator*, October, 1992

Question:

Can you continue to strive for perfection, but not become obsessed with your striving?

Excellence from Matthew 5:48

Be perfect, therefore, as your heavenly Father is perfect.

Take A Risk

To laugh is to risk appearing the fool.
To weep is to risk appearing sentimental.
To reach out for another is to risk involvement.
To expose feelings is to risk exposing our true self.
To place your ideas, your dreams, before the crowd is to risk loss.
To love is to risk not being loved in return.
To live is to risk dying.
To hope is to risk despair.
To try at all is to risk failure.
But risk we must, because the greatest hazard in life is to risk nothing.
The man, the woman, who risks nothing does nothing, has nothing, and is nothing.

– Author Unknown

Question:

What risk is God directing you to take?

Excellence from Hebrews 10:38

But my righteous one will live by faith. And if he shrinks back, I will not be pleased with him.

Take Responsibility

THIS IS A STORY ABOUT FOUR PEOPLE named Everybody, Somebody, Anybody and Nobody. There was an important job to be done and Everybody was sure that Somebody would do it. Anybody could have done it, but Nobody did it. Somebody got angry about that, because it was Everybody's job. Everybody thought Anybody could do it, but Nobody realized that Everybody wouldn't do it. It ended up that Everybody blamed Somebody when Nobody did what Anybody could have done!

–Author Unknown

Question:

What responsibility could you assume that needs to be done but isn't getting done?

Excellence from Ephesians 5:15-16

> *Be very careful, then how you live — not as unwise but as wise, making the most of every opportunity, because the days are evil.*

Trust God

YEARS AGO A LITTLE GIRL in a small Pennsylvania town fell into an abandoned mine shaft. Though the diggings had been covered for years, in time the boards had rotted and the weight of the girl caused them to give way. She fell into the dark, deep pit.

People from the village gathered to form a plan to rescue the girl now lying at the bottom of the mine. They could hear her cry out, so they knew she was alive. Hope surged through the tense crowd and through the broken hearts of her parents.

One old miner suggested that they find a small child that could be lowered through the opening where the girl had fallen, letting this second child take along another rope to affix to the fallen one. Strong men could then lift both children back to safety.

They found such a small child. She was a close friend of the girl in the mine. She agreed to go down. Her mother also gave her permission. The crowd cheered the girl's bravery. However, as she approached the mouth of the mine, she became afraid and refused to go down.

She removed the rope around her waist and ran home. The crew was afraid to try any other method of freeing the girl at the bottom of the shaft. If they tried to remove the rock and dirt to make the entryway bigger, some additional debris would be bound to fall on her. So they began to search for another small child.

Their search was soon over, for the girl who had offered to be lowered before came running back in the company of a man. She approached the men who held the ropes and agreed to go down. Looking into the faces of those strong men, she made one request, "I'll go down, but I want my father to hold the rope."

The man with her, her father, could not have been any stronger than the other men there; but she had great confidence that with her father holding the rope, she would be safe and secure. The plan worked, and the little girl at the bottom of the shaft was saved.

How often in our lives we find ourselves holding onto ropes that are not secure. There are so many available ropes in this permissive society — fame, fortune, success, winning games, popularity, peer pressure, dope, booze, illicit sex, and most of all, SELF. But none of these things provide lasting security.

We need to grasp the rope that our Father holds! How secure it is! He will never fail us. We can be lowered to any depth and feel safe if our Father holds the rope of our lives.

– Dan Stavely

Question:

Who holds the rope in your life?

Excellence from Deuteronomy 33:27

The eternal God is your refuge, and underneath are the everlasting arms.

Value Character

"FAME IS A VAPOR, popularity an accident, riches take wings, those who cheer today will curse tomorrow, only one thing remains — character!"

– Horrace Greeley
on his deathbed

Question:

Is character more important to you than money or fame?

Excellence from Philippians 1:27

Whatever happens, conduct yourselves in a manner worthy of the gospel of Christ.

Value Freedom Over Security

ONCE UPON A TIME in the long, long ago the Eagle and the Chicken were very good friends. Everywhere they went these friends went together. It was not uncommon for people to look up and see the Eagle and the Chicken flying side by side through the air.

One day while flying, the Chicken said to the Eagle: "Let's drop down and get a bite to eat. My stomach is growling."

Sounds like a good idea to me," replied the Eagle. So the two birds glided down to earth, saw several animals eating, and decided to join them. They landed next to the Cow. The Cow was busy eating corn, but noticed that the Eagle and the Chicken were soon sitting on the ground next to her. "Welcome," said the Cow. "Help yourself to the corn."

This took the two birds by surprise. They were not accustomed to having other animals share their food quite so readily. "Why are you willing to share your corn with us?" asked the Eagle.

"Oh, we have plenty to eat here. Mr. Farmer gives us all we want," replied the Cow. Well, the Eagle and the Chicken jumped in and ate their fill. When they finished, the Chicken asked more about Mr. Farmer.

"Well, said the Cow, "he grows all our food. We don't have to work for the food at all."

"You mean," said the Chicken, "that Mr. Farmer simply gives you all you want to eat?"

"That's right," said the Cow. "Now only that, but he gives us shelter over our heads." The Chicken and the Eagle were shocked! They had never heard of such a thing. They had always had to search for food and work for shelter.

When it came time to leave, the Chicken and the Eagle began to discuss the situation. "Maybe we should just stay here," said the Chicken. "We can have all the food we want without working. And that barn over there sure beats those nests we have been building. Besides, I'm getting tired of always having to work for a living."

"I don't know about all this," said the Eagle. "It sounds too good to be true. I find it hard to believe that one can get something for nothing. Besides, I kinda like flying high and free through the air. And providing for food and shelter isn't so bad. In fact, I find it quite challenging.

81

Well, the Chicken thought it over and decided to stay where there was free food and shelter. But the Eagle decided that he loved his freedom too much to give it up, and enjoyed the consistent challenge of making his own living. So, after saying goodbye to his old friend the Chicken, the Eagle set sail for the wild blue yonder.

Everything went fine for the Chicken. He ate all he wanted. He never worked. He grew fat and lazy. But then one day he heard the farmer say to his wife that the preacher was coming to visit the next day and they should have fried chicken for dinner. Hearing that, the Chicken decided it was time to check out and rejoin his good friend Mr. Eagle. But when he attempted to fly he found that he had grown too fat and lazy. Instead of being able to fly, he could only flutter. So the next day the farmer's family and the preacher sat down to fried Chicken.

When you give up the challenges of life in pursuit of security, you give up your freedom.

– Don Wildmon

Question:
What freedoms have you given up in pursuit of security?

Excellence from Proverbs 14:12

> *There is a way that seems right to a man, but in the end it leads to death.*

Value Friendships

DURING THE CIVIL WAR, nineteen-year-old Sam Davis wrote the following letter to his Mom and Dad:

> "Dear Mom and Dad,
>   Tomorrow I will be hanged. It's nothing you've done, but I've gotten into trouble here in the war and they're going to hang me.
>
Love, Sam."

What events led to Sam Davis' hanging? Sam was a young Confederate spy. He was assigned to go behind the lines of the Union army and gather information. On one such spy mission, he ran into another nineteen-year-old from the Union army and they became friends.

Those two nineteen-year-old friends stayed together for several days. Soon the Union soldier told Sam to go back to his army. As he left, the Union soldier gave Sam some maps of Union troop movements. He said, "Sam, these maps are no longer accurate, but put them into your saddlebags and take them to your general. They'll think you did a good job over here and give you a promotion." Sam probably laughed to himself as he raced back toward the front line. He was captured abruptly by a Union guard. As the guard went through his saddlebags he found the maps. "Where'd you get the maps, son?" he asked Sam Davis.

"I'm, not going to tell you" replied Sam.

"You'll tell us all right!" said the guard. He took Sam to jail. After a few days passed, the hanging gallows were set up for the Confederate soldier's hanging. They came to his cell to get him and made him ride to the gallows on his coffin which was secured to the back of a horse-drawn wagon. When he got to the gallows a Union general approached the frightened young teenager. "What's your name, son?"

"Sam Davis, Sir."

"Do you see those gallows? They're here for you."

"Yes, Sir."

"If you tell me where you got the maps I won't hang you."

"I can't tell you."

"What do you mean you can't tell me. Didn't you hear what I just offered you?"

"I got the maps from a friend and I'm not going to tell you who he is."

"Look, son," the general looked intently into the teenager's eyes, "you're nineteen years old and have a long life ahead of you. I don't want to hang you. I just want to know where you got the maps. If you'll just tell me who gave them to you, I'll personally escort you back across the lines to safety. Where did you get the maps?"

With the boldness of a fifty-year-old warrior, Sam Davis looked into the general's face and said, ""Sir, I'd die a thousand deaths before I'd deny my friend and I'm disappointed you asked me to do that."

Question:

What kind of a friend are you?

Excellence from Proverbs 17:17

A friend loves at all times, and a brother is born for adversity.

Excellence Illustrated

Value the Best Above the Good

ONE NIGHT IN 1994, CHUCK BELK had an alarming dream. He was
driving a truck which transported a precious cargo. The road
was winding and hazardous, but Chuck was doing a good job.
Potholes made the ride a rough one and the elevation in-
creased with each mile. Still, he persisted skillfully and faithfully. Finally, the road became so narrow and rocky it was
impossible to drive another mile. In his dream, Chuck got out
of the cab, loaded the precious cargo into a large bag, and
continued up the mountain with the heavy load on his back.
The heavy load fatigued him as he lugged it up the steep
incline. Just as he reached the summit and began to enjoy
the majestic view of the valley below, a creature with a most
hideous face stepped out from behind a large boulder,
stretched out his hands, and with a smirking smile said,
"Thank you very much."

Chuck awoke with a start. His heart was pounding and he
broke into a cold sweat.

"What does this mean, Lord?" he asked.

Instantly, Chuck felt impressed that the journey was his
lifetime, the hideous creature was Satan, and the precious
cargo was all the good things he had done throughout his
lifetime.

As Satan stole all his good works, God was saying to
Chuck that it was those good things he did on his own that
stood in the way of the best things *God wanted to do* through
him in his lifetime!

Is the good in your life standing in the way of God's best?
If so, drop your own agenda and let Him do what He wants
with your life. When you reach the end of the journey, you'll
be glad you did.

Question:

What good things are standing in the way of the best
things in life?

Excellence from Matthew 6:33

> But seek first his kingdom and his righteousness, and all
> these things will be given to you as well.

85

Value True Riches I

A MAN VISITED A CERTAIN HOME. The home wasn't much to look at, kinda run down and lacking even a good coat of paint. Outside the home, in the yard, a little boy and his sister were playing. They were laughing, running, and having a good time. The man surveyed the situation and concluded that the family wasn't very well off.

He asked the small boy some questions about the home and family. The little boy told him that his father had not been able to work lately because of illness and that his mother had to care for the father. When asked about his patched clothes and his bare feet, the youngster explained that he had not had any new clothes since his daddy got sick. After a long period of conversation, the visiting gentleman found out that the little boy and his sister had not been to a movie, or to get a cone of ice cream, or any of the normally accepted childhood pleasures for several months. Wanting to say something to help the boy and his sister face the difficult situation, the man spoke. "It must be awful bad to be poor." Quick as a flash the youngster answered back. "Mister, we ain't poor. We just ain't got no money."

How true! How eternally true! He was happy. He loved his sister. His parents loved him. He knew why his family was in the shape it was in financially and he didn't complain. Money could not have bought what he had.

– Don Wildmon

Question:

How is a person truly made rich?

Excellence from Luke 12:23

Life is more than food, and the body more than clothes.

86

Value True Riches II

Money will buy a bed
    but not sleep;
books
    but not brains;
food
    but not appetite;
finery
    but not beauty;
a house
    but not a home;
medicine
    but not health;
luxuries
    but not culture;
amusements
    but not happiness;
religion
    but not salvation;
a passport to everywhere
    but heaven.
                – The Voice in the Wilderness

Question:

What is really important in your life?

Excellence from Isaiah 55:2

Why spend money on what is not bread, and your labor on what does not satisfy.

Win Fairly

KNUTE ROCKNE WAS FAMOUS for his use of words in motivating his football teams. He also gave a great speech one day on "Athletics and Leadership," in which he talked about the will to win. Rockne said,

> "Some of you may say, this will to win is a bad thing. In what way is it a bad thing? Education is supposed to prepare a young man for life. Life is competition. Success in life goes only to the man who competes successfully. A successful lawyer is the man who goes out and wins — wins law cases. A successful physician is a man who goes out and wins — saves lives and restores men to health. A successful sales manager is a man who goes out and wins — sells the goods. The successful executive is the man who can make money and stay out of the bankruptcy court. There is no reward for the loser. There is nothing wrong with the will to win. The only penalty should be that the man who wins unfairly should be set down."

Question:

Do you play the game of life to win fairly and decently?

Excellence from Ephesians 5:11

Have nothing to do with the fruitless deeds of darkness, but rather expose them.

Win in Life

WINNERS TAKE CHANCES. Like everyone else, they fear failing, but they refuse to let fear control them. Winners don't give up. When life gets rough, they hang in until the going gets better. Winners are flexible. They realize there is more than one way and are willing to try others. Winners know they are not perfect. They respect their weaknesses while making the most of their strengths. Winners fall, but they don't stay down. They stubbornly refuse to let a fall keep them from climbing. Winners don't blame fate for their failures, nor luck for their successes. Winners accept responsibility for their lives. Winners are positive thinkers who see good in all things. From the ordinary, they make the extraordinary. Winners believe in the path they have chosen even when it is hard, even when others can't see where they are going. Winners are patient. They know a goal is only as worthy as the effort that's required to achieve it. Winners are people like you. They make this world a better place to be.

— Nancy Sims

Question:

Are you winning in the game of life?

Excellence from 1 Corinthians 9:27

Do you not know that in a race all the runners run, but only one gets the prize? Run in such a way as to get the prize.

Win One Person to Christ

A SUNDAY SCHOOL TEACHER, Ezra Kimball, in 1858 led a Boston shoe clerk to Christ. The clerk, D. L. Moody, became an evangelist and in 1879 awakened evangelistic zeal in the heart of Frederick B. Meyer, pastor of a small church.

F. B. Meyer, preaching on an American college campus, brought to Christ a student named J. Wilbur Chapman. Chapman engaged in YMCA work and employed a former baseball player, Billy Sunday, to do evangelistic work.

Sunday held a revival in Charlotte, North Carolina. A group of local men were so enthusiastic afterward that they planned another campaign, bringing Mordecai Hamm to town to preach.

In the revival, a young man named Billy Graham heard the Gospel and yielded his life to Christ. Billy Graham . . . and the story goes on and on . . .

Question:

Will you ask God for the opening to win one person to Christ?

Excellence from 2 Corinthians 5:20

We are therefore Christ's ambassadors, as though God were making his appeal through us. We implore you on Christ's behalf: be reconciled to God.

EXCELLENCE ILLUSTRATED
By Humor

"A cheerful heart is good medicine."
Proverbs 17:22

Avoid Complaining

A MONK WAS ASSIGNED to a medieval monastery and told to work hard in silence. He was only allowed to speak once a year and then was limited to two words. After one year the monk was called in to his Father Superior and asked how the year had been.

"Bed hard," he replied.

After a second year he was again called before his Superior for a comment.

"Food cold," was his statement.

Another year passed and he was called in for a third conference.

"I quit," the monk said as he walked out.

His Superior replied, "Well, I'm not surprised. You've done nothing but complain since you got here anyway!"

Be Careful How You Jest

A FOOTBALL COACH AND A BASKETBALL COACH loved to hunt and were invited by a parent to come to his farm to hunt quail. So, when their seasons were over, they jumped in the car and drove 50 miles to his land. Arriving at the farm house, the football coach said, "I'll go in and ask where we should hunt. You stay here and I'll be back."

The football coach was greeted cordially and told where to find quail. As he turned to leave, the farmer said, "There's just one thing I'd like you to do for me if you're going to hunt on my land. Did you see that old mule out in the yard when you came in?'

"Yes," said the football coach.

"I want you to shoot my mule. He's been a family pet, but he's so old and sick he needs to be put out of his misery. None of us can do it."

"I don't want to shoot your mule," replied the coach.

"You must," said the farmer.

"Okay," said the coach, "if that's what you really want, I'll do it."

On the way back to the car, the football coach decided to have some fun with the basketball coach.

"That old killjoy," he said to his friend in the car. "We came all the way out here to hunt quail and now he won't let us hunt on his land. I'm so mad I'm going to shoot his mule."

With that, the football coach raised his gun and dropped the animal.

Before he could turn around, he heard two more shots.

"Let's get out of here," said the basketball coach, "I just got two of his cows."

Be Careful Who You Tell

A YOUNG COUNTRY BOY had asked a very good looking young lady for his first date. He went to town to get her a gift and entered the drug store on the corner.

"I'd like three boxes of your best Whitman's Sampler candy," he told the druggist. "Give me a one-pound box, a two-pound box, and a five-pound box."

Curious, the druggist asked why he needed three boxes.

"Well," he replied. "I have a date tonight with a pretty girl. If I can hold her hand, I'm giving her the one-pound box. If she lets me give her a hug, she'll get the two-pound box. But if she lets me give her a kiss, I'm giving her the five-pound box of candy before I take her home."

That night, the young man went to dinner in the home of his girl. He left the candy outside on the porch swing. The father asked him to pray before the meal and he prayed for *seven* minutes! He thanked God for the sun, moon and stars, prayed for all the relatives, and for every country he could think of.

After supper, the boy and the young girl were sitting outside on the porch swing.

"I didn't know you were so religious," she said.

He replied, "I didn't know your father was a druggist!"

Excellence Illustrated

Be Flexible

A WOMAN WHO WAS CALLED to jury duty told the presiding judge
that she was not qualified to serve because she did not believe
in capital punishment. The judge said, "You don't understand,
madam. This is a civil case involving a man who spent five
thousand dollars of his wife's money on gambling and other
women." To which the woman replied eagerly, "I'll be happy to
serve, your honor, and I've changed my mind about capital
punishment."

Excellence Illustrated

Believe God's Word

A LITTLE BOY LEFT SUNDAY SCHOOL with a picture of Jonah and the
great fish. On his way home, he met a man who said, "You
don't believe that nonsense about Jonah and the whale, do
you?"

"Sure," replied the boy. "It's in the Bible."

"How do you know it's true, just because it's in the Bible,"
asked the man.

"Well, I'll ask Jonah when I get to Heaven," said the youth.

"What if Jonah isn't in Heaven? asked the man.

"Then you ask him, mister," said the boy.

Excellence Illustrated

Be Optimistic

A FARMER WAS CONTINUALLY OPTIMISTIC, seldom discouraged or blue.
He had a neighbor who was just the opposite. Grim and
gloomy, he faced each new morning with a heavy sigh.

The happy, optimistic farmer would see the sun coming
up and shout over the roar of the tractor, "Look at that beautiful sun and the clear sky!" And with a frown, the negative
neighbor would reply, "Yeah — it'll probably scorch the crops!"

When clouds would gather and much-needed rain would
start to fall, our positive friend would smile across the fence,
"Ain't this great — God is giving our corn a drink today!"
Again, the same negative response, " Uh Huh . . . but if it
doesn't stop 'fore long it'll flood and wash everything away."

One day the optimist decided to put his pessimistic neighbor to the maximum test. He bought the smartest, most
expensive bird dog he could find. He trained him to do things
no other dog on earth could do — impossible feats that would
surely astound anyone.

He invited the pessimist to go duck hunting with him.
They sat in the boat, hidden in the duck blind. In came the
ducks. Both men fired and several ducks fell into the water.
"Go get 'em!" ordered the owner with a gleam in his eye. The
dog leaped out of the boat, walked on the water, and picked
up the birds one by one.

"Well, what do ya think of that?" asked the optimist.

Unsmiling, the pessimist answered, "He can't swim, can
he?"

97

Excellence Illustrated

Don't Be Self-Centered

A MAN WAS SO SELF-CENTERED in his prayers, he said to God,
"Lord, You're so big and can do so much, a minute to You is
like a million years."

"Right," replied the Lord.

"A penny to You is like a million dollars, isn't it?" added
the man.

"Right," replied the Lord again.

"Lord, can I have a penny?" asked the man.

"Wait a minute," said the Lord.

Excellence Illustrated

Don't Believe Everything You're Told

Two CITY SLICKERS had never been out of New York City. They decided that they had had it with city living, so they bought a ranch down in Texas in order to live off the land like their ancestors.

The first thing they decided they needed was a mule. So they went to a neighboring rancher and asked him if he had a mule to sell. The rancher answered, "No, I'm afraid not."

They were disappointed, but as they visited with the rancher for a few moments one of them saw some honeydew melons stacked against the barn and asked, "What are those?" The rancher, seeing that they were from the city decided to have some fun. "Oh," he answered, "those are mule eggs. You take one of those eggs home and wait for it to hatch, and you'll have a mule." The city slickers were overjoyed at this, so they bought one of the melons and headed down the bumpy country road toward their own ranch. Suddenly they hit an especially treacherous bump, and the honeydew melon bounced out the back of the pickup truck, hit the road, and burst open. Now, seeing in the rearview mirror what had happened, the driver turned his truck around and drove back to see if he could retrieve his mule egg.

Meanwhile, a big old Texas jackrabbit came hopping by and saw this honeydew melon burst in the road. He hopped over to it and, standing in the middle of that mess, he began to eat. Now here came the two city slickers. They spied their mule egg burst open and this long-eared creature in the middle of it. One of the men shouted, "Our mule egg has hatched! Let's get our mule."

But seeing those two men coming toward it, the jackrabbit took off hopping in every direction with the two city fellows in hot pursuit. The two men from New York gave everything they had to catch him, but finally they could go no farther. Both men fell wearily onto the ground gasping for air while the jackrabbit hopped off into the distance. Raising up on his elbow, one of the men said to the other, "Well, I guess we lost our mule." The other man nodded grimly. "Yes, but you know," he said, "I'm not sure I wanted to plow that fast anyway."

Don't Expect A Quick Fix

A FAMILY OF COUNTRY FOLKS from way back in the woods came to town and pulled up in front of a fancy hotel. The backwoods father and husband jumped out of the car with his two boys to reserve a room. His wife stayed in the car.

Now these men-folks had never seen an elevator before, and as they entered the hotel, an elevator door opened to admit a rather obese, untidy matron. A few seconds later, as the country boys stood at the front desk, the elevator returned, the door opened, and a young, attractive career girl in her twenties stepped out.

With eyes as big as saucers, the old woodsman exclaimed to his sons, "Quick boys, go get your Ma. We'll run her through that thing."

Follow Instructions

WITH HIS FIRST AND SECOND STRING quarterbacks injured, a high school football coach was forced to use his third stringer in the fourth quarter of a tie game. Reasoning that a tie was better than a loss, the coach summoned the boy alongside him.

"We're on our own 20-yard line," said the coach. "Go into the game, run three plays, hold unto the ball, and then punt the ball."

On the first play, the young quarterback gained 20 yards on a run around the left end. Then he gained 30 yards around right end. On the third play he caught the defense napping and gained 20 more yards on a sneak. With the ball now on the opponents 10-yard line, he then punted the ball out of the end zone as time expired.

After the game, the coach grabbed the third-string QB and demanded, "What in the world were you thinking about, punting the ball in that situation?"

"I was thinking what a dumb coach we have," replied the boy.

Get Adequate Sleep

WHEN I WAS A BOY BACK HOME ON THE FARM, once we had a blizzard. Of course, when we had that kind of weather, the schools would shut down. So they closed the schools for three days. Then, on the first day school was open, the teacher noticed my friend on the front row with his head on his desk, sound asleep. She woke him up and said, "What's the matter? Why are you sleeping in school? Are you sick?"

The boy said, "No, I'm not sick. I just didn't get any sleep last night. It was the chicken thieves. You know, they've been stealing our chickens for a long time and Pa said the next time they came around he was going to get himself a couple of dead chicken thieves. Last night in the middle of the night he heard 'em. So Pa jumped out of bed and ran for the chicken house. He didn't even take time to put on his trousers. He ran out in his nightshirt. He grabbed his shotgun by the back door and loaded both barrels. He put his fingers on both triggers and he tiptoed out through all that snow to the chicken house. He heard 'em inside and he was easing that door open real careful like with his gun pointed inside. Well, you know that old dog of ours named Towser? He came up behind Pa with his cold nose. And we were up all night long last night picking and cleaning chickens."

Get Motivated

THERE WAS A YOUNG MAN who took a short cut home late one night through the cemetery. He fell into an open grave. He called for help and he tried to climb out, but all to no avail. There was no one around to hear his cries or lend a hand. So he settled down for the night in a corner of the darkened grave to await morning. A little while later another person came along the same route through the cemetery, taking the same short cut home. He, too, fell into the grave. He started clawing and shouting and trying to get out just as the first man had done. Suddenly, the second fellow heard a voice out of the dark corner of the grave saying, "You can't get out of here."

But he did!

Gracefully Share Bad News

A MAN WAS OUT OF TOWN on a trip and he asked his brother to take care of his cat while he was away. The cat was a beautiful Siamese and meant a great deal to the man, although the brother who was caring for the cat didn't like cats at all. When he got back from the trip he called his brother's house and asked about his cat. The brother was very curt, and replied, "Your cat died." And then he hung up. For days the man was inconsolable. Finally, he phoned his brother again to point out, "It was needlessly cruel and sadistic of you to tell me so bluntly that my poor cat had passed away."

The brother demanded, "Well, what did you expect me to do?"

The cat-lover said, "Well, you could have broken the bad news to me gradually. First, you could have said the cat was playing on the roof. Later you could have called to say he fell off. The next morning you could have reported he had broken his leg. Then, when I came to get him, you could have told me he had passed away during the night. But you didn't have it in you to be that civilized. Now tell me — how's Mama?"

The brother pondered momentarily, then announced, "She's playing on the roof."

Handle Job Stress

COACH JONES WAS NOT FEELING WELL. There was nothing specific that he could complain of — just some vague aches and pains, and a general feeling of not being quite right. Finally, he decided to pay a visit to his doctor.

The physician examined him thoroughly, and proclaimed him to be in excellent health.

"Then why do I feel so poorly all the time?" the coach asked.

"Well," answered the doctor, "you have a very stressful job. We're just beginning to learn that stress can produce some very bad effects on people. I would say that the stress you undergo every day is taking a toll on your physical well-being. That's why you don't feel well."

"If that's the case," asked the coach, "what can I do about it?"

The doctor smiled kindly and said, "It's really very simple. For the next few weeks, I want you to relax completely. Forget about coaching; forget about the team; forget about winning and losing. Just stay calm and avoid all situations that could upset you or cause you any kind of stress."

"Thank you, Doctor," said Coach Jones. "I'll try. I'm not going to get upset, and I'll avoid all unpleasant situations."

"Good," smiled the doctor. "Oh, by the way, there's one more thing I'd like to ask you."

"Certainly, Doctor," said the coach. "What is it?"

"Well," said the doctor as he frowned deeply, "during the game last Saturday when we were fourth and seven on our own thirty-five-yard line, why did you go for it? Are you some kind of idiot?"

Honesty

AN OLD MISER called his doctor, lawyer, and pastor to his death-bed.

"They say you can't take it with you," the dying man said, "but I'm going to. I've got three envelopes with $30,000 cash in each one. I want each of you to take one and just when they lower my casket, you throw in the envelope."

At the funeral each man tossed in his envelope. On the way home, the pastor confessed, "I needed the money for the church so I took out $10,000 and threw only $20,000 into the grave."

The doctor said, "I, too, must confess. I'm building a clinic. So, I took $20,000 and threw in only $10,000."

The lawyer said, "Gentlemen, I'm ashamed of you. I threw in a check for the full amount."

–Shelby W. Adkins

Learn Your Lessons from Trials

A CHRISTIAN LADY wanted a parrot that could talk. She looked in several shops before finding one. The owner told her, however, that the parrot had been previously owned by a bartender and though he could say anything, he also on occasion used profanity. She told him she would buy him anyway and teach him to say good things. Everything went well for about a month. He learned to say "Praise the Lord" and a number of other Christian words and phrases. One day she forgot to feed him and when she came into the house she heard him cursing. She grabbed him up and said, "I told you not to talk that way. I'll teach you never to do it again." So she put him in the deep freeze and shut the door. A few minutes later she took him out and asked, "Have you learned your lesson?" The bird shivered and replied, "Yes, ma'am." She asked, "Are you going to talk that way anymore?" The parrot replied, "No, ma'am."

About seven months went by and not a bit of bad language. Apparently the bird was cured of his rascally habits. Then one day she forgot to feed him, water him, or change his cage. When she returned home that day he was carrying on worse than ever. She grabbed him and put him back in the freezer, but forgot him for some time. He was almost frozen to death when she thought of him. She put him in his cage to thaw out. Finally he began to move and talk a little and she asked him again, "Did you learn your lesson?" "Yes, ma'am" he retorted. He sat there quietly for a few more minutes shivering. Finally he said, "Can I ask you a question?" She answered, "Yes." The parrot said, "I thought I knew all the bad words there were, but just what did that turkey in there say?"

Pay Attention

A YOUNG MINISTER was making his first hospital visit to an intensive care patient. Tubes were running into and out of the oxygen tent as the pastor read a Psalm of comfort. With labored effort, the patient feebly scrawled a note to the pastor, collapsed in the bed, and died.

Stunned by the experience the pastor stuffed the note in his pocket as hospital attendants attempted unsuccessfully to revive the patient.

The next day, still shocked at the sudden death of the church member, the minister remembered the note, pulled it from his pocket, and read, "Please don't stand on my oxygen hose!"

Read Between the Lines

A MAN WALKED into a pet shop. He was greeted by a talking parrot who said, "You are the ugliest man I've ever met."

Offended, the man found the owner of the store and complained.

The owner reached inside the cage, grabbed the bird by the neck and took him into the bathroom. He slapped him on one side of the beak after the other as feathers flew and the parrot squawked.

Returning him to his cage, the man said, "Now, I never want to hear you say anyone is 'the ugliest person you've ever met,' again.

"Okay," said the bird. The owner returned to his duties.

Satisfied, the customer turned to go out the door.

"Hey, mister," said the parrot.

"What?" said the man as he turned around.

"You know," said the parrot.

Remember

A MAN AND HIS WIFE were visiting Santa Fe, New Mexico. As they were strolling through the market where the Indians have all of their handicrafts displayed, they came to an old Indian who was sitting on his blanket being questioned by a dozen or so people who had gathered around.

"This old man has a 100 percent memory," someone said. "Ask him something. He remembers everything and everybody."

The man waited his turn and then said to the Indian, "What did you have for breakfast on November 27, 1942."

The Indian looked at him and said one word, "Eggs."

The man turned and said to his wife, "He's a fraud. Everybody eats eggs for breakfast. He's just being clever."

Four years later the man and his wife were back in Santa Fe. And there sat that same old Indian. Wanting to be friendly, the man rushed over to him, raised his right hand and said, "How!"

The Indian looked at him for a moment and said, "Over light."

Remember Who You Are

A CONVENTION SPEAKER LOOKED OVER HIS AUDIENCE before speaking and said, "Excuse me for taking that extra few seconds but I was looking to see if Mr. Pie was able to get to the meeting. As I got on the elevator in the lobby earlier today, there were half a dozen men and women on it. One man was wearing one of your convention badges. When the elevator stopped at the mezzanine floor an attractive young lady stepped in. Immediately she moved up close to this man and patted him on the cheek and said, 'Hi, Sweetie Pie.' And the lady standing next to him put out her hand to the young lady and said, 'I'm so glad to meet you — I'm Mrs. Pie.'"

Set Realistic Goals

TWO HUNTERS went out to shoot rabbits with .22 caliber rifles. One hunter saw a bear and foolishly stung him with a shot. As the bear charged, the second hunter kicked off his boots.

"Why are you doing that?" panicked the first hunter. "You know you can't outrun that bear."

"I don't have to," replied the second hunter. "I just have to outrun you!"

Stay Humble

THE LION WAS PROUD of his mastery of the animal kingdom. One day he decided to make sure all the other animals knew he was the king of the jungle. He was so confident that he by-passed the smaller animals and went straight to the bear. "Who is the king of the jungle?" the lion asked. The bear replied, "Why, you are, of course." The lion gave a mighty roar of approval.

Next he asked the tiger, "Who is the king of the jungle?" The tiger quickly responded, "Everyone knows that you are, O mighty lion."

Next on the list was the elephant. The lion faced the elephant and addressed his question: "Who is the king of the jungle?" The elephant immediately grabbed the lion with his trunk, whirled him around in the air five or six times, and slammed him into a tree. Then he pounded him onto the ground several times, dunked him under water in a nearby lake, and finally threw him up on the shore.

The lion — beaten, bruised, and battered — struggled to his feet. He looked at the elephant through sad and bloody eyes and said, "Look, just because you don't know the answer is no reason for you to get mean about it."

Teamwork

KEN, AN ELDERLY GOLFER, was losing his eyesight. He hadn't played for several months, but wanted to get to the course again. A friend introduced him to Bill, an 80-year-old man who couldn't play a lick but had eyes like a hawk. They teamed up for a round of golf.

Ken teed up and hit the ball.

"Did you see where it went?" he asked.

"Yup," replied Bill.

"Well, where is it?" demanded Ken.

"I forgot," said Bill.

Think Fast

JOE ONCE HAD A NEW JOB as a stockroom boy in a grocery. He was a "hippie type," with long hair, tight jeans and an earring. One day a little old lady, a frugal type who bought only what she needed approached Joe.

"I'll have 1/2 head of lettuce." she said.

"I'll have to ask my boss," said Joe.

Joe went back to the storeroom and said, "some tightwad out there wants to buy 1/2 head of lettuce." What Joe didn't know was that the woman was right behind him. He saw her and quickly added, "and here's the dear lady who wants to buy the other half!"

Joe's boss kindly dismissed both, but said he'd like to see Joe after work. Joe came by and the boss said, "I admire a man who thinks on his feet, but you don't seem to be from around here."

Joe said, "I'm not. I'm from Aliquippa, Pennsylvania, and we're known for two things; our hockey teams and for having the ugliest girls in the world."

"Very interesting," said the boss. "My wife is from Alliquipa."

"Oh really," said Joe. "And which team did she play for?

Use Your Head

A FOOTBALL COACH AND A BASKETBALL COACH were arguing over who had the dumbest athlete. "Let's bet on it," said the basketball coach. So they did.
The football coach called in his star lineman and said, "Butch, take this quarter and go downtown and buy me a Cadillac."

"Sure," said Butch.

"Now, did you ever see anyone so naive?" the football coach asked the basketball coach.

"That's nothing. Watch this," replied the basketball coach.

"Clyde," he said to his basketball player. "Go down to my office and see if I'm in."

"Okay, coach," replied Clyde.

"Well, I guess you win," said the football coach. "That was pretty dumb."

Meanwhile the football player met the basketball player in the hallway. "You wouldn't believe how dumb my coach is," said the football player. "He told me to buy a Cadillac with a quarter and didn't even say what color to get!"

"How about my coach," said the basketball player. "He said to go to his office to see if he's in. All he had to do was pick up the phone, call down, and see for himself."

Value Every Friend

PEPPER RODGERS says he was having a hard time in coaching. He felt all alone. So he said to his wife, "My dog is about my only friend and a man needs at least two friends in life."

"So, she bought me another dog," he groaned.

Value Love Over Money

A YOUNG MAN PROPOSED to his girl as they sat looking over a beautiful lake. "Darling, I want you to know that I love you more than anything else in the world. I want you to marry me. I'm not wealthy. I don't have a Rolls-Royce like Johnny Green, but I do love you with all my heart."

She thought for a minute and then replied, "I love you with all my heart, too, but tell me more about Johnny Green."

EXCELLENCE ILLUSTRATED
with Object Lessons

"Now these things occured as examples . . . ."
1 Corinthians 10:6

A Clean Mind

WE CANNOT STOP EVIL THOUGHTS from entering our minds occasionally, any more than we can keep birds from flying overhead. But we can stop a bird from building a nest in our hair!

Every time a bad thought enters your mind, "frisk it" like a policeman frisks a suspect. Mentally determine who originated that thought and whether it pleases God. If it came from self or Satan, discard it immediately.

Excellence from Philippians 4:8

Finally, brothers, whatever is true, whatever is noble, whatever is right, whatever is pure, whatever is lovely, whatever is admirable — if anything is excellent or praiseworthy — think about such things.

Assurance of Salvation

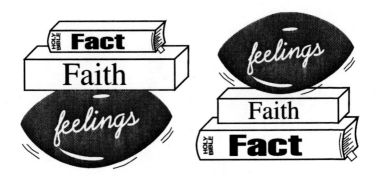

HAVE YOU ACCEPTED JESUS as your personal Savior? If so, you have eternal life, based upon the fact that God promises to save you forever. He will never leave you and he will never let you go (1 John 5:11-13; John 5:24, 6:37-40, 10:27-30).

Feelings may come and go.

You must place your faith in the fact that God and His Word are trustworthy. You must not trust feelings. Only then will you live a stable, consistent life.

Excellence from Psalm 119:89

Your word, O Lord, is eternal; it stands firm in the heavens.

Movies, Magazines, and Music

HOLD A CUP OF WATER with one hand. Ask a volunteer to shake your hand at the wrist. Keep shaking. If no water spills, ask him to shake harder. Then pose the question, "Why did water come out of the cup?"

Someone will say, "Because he shook your hand."

But the real reason water came out of the cup is that water was in the cup in the first place.

All of us will be shaken. What comes out of our lives (how we act) depends upon what we have put in our minds. Be careful what you watch, read, and hear. From which perspective does it come, God's or this world's?

Excellence from Romans 12:2

Do not conform any longer to the pattern of this world, but be transformed by the renewing of your mind.

Our Need of Jesus

WHAT IS THIS BASEBALL GLOVE capable of doing? NOTHING, by itself! It has great potential, but only when put on a hand. Put it on. Now what can it do? It can do all it was intended to do. It can be used to signal another player, catch fly balls, and field ground balls. Its purpose is now fulfilled.

We need Jesus to come into our lives to enable us to do all we were created to do. Our potential and purpose in life is fulfilled only in Him.

Excellence from John 15:5

Apart from me, you can do nothing.

Priorities

FILL A SMALL (5" diameter) CAN with baseballs. Then pour marbles in and around the baseballs until the can is packed to capacity. This can represents a life that is full of everything God intends.

Remove both baseballs and marbles. Now put the marbles in first and then as many baseballs as possible. They won't all fit! Why? Because you didn't take care of the big things, the most important things in life first. Little things are important, but be sure to take care of priorities first!

Excellence from Matthew 6:25

Therefore I tell you, do not worry about your life, what you will eat or drink; or about your body, what you will wear. Is not life more important than food, and the body more important than clothes?

Purity

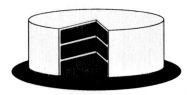

PLAY THE ROLE OF "CAKE-BAKER."

One by one, add necessary ingredients to make a good cake to a pan. (sugar, cake mix, milk, eggs, salt, flavoring, baking powder, etc.).

Next bring out some pickle juice, catsup, or taco sauce (or all three!). Should these be added to make a good cake? Add them!

The right ingredients (God's Word, church attendance, prayer) make for a sweet tasting, successful life. The wrong ingredients (filthy movies, alcohol and drugs, sexual sins) added to a life make it impure and spoil the result.

Excellence from 1 Peter 1:15

But just as he who called you is holy, so be holy in all you do.

Rest in Him

Put an egg under a frying pan and hit the pan as hard as you can with something like a hammer. We are the egg. We are weak and fragile people. The pan is Christ Jesus, God's protection. We are "in Christ" by faith. The blows of life cannot crack us because we abide in Him!

Excellence from Psalm 91:1

He who dwells in the shelter of the Most High will rest in the shadow of the Almighty.

Salvation

GRASP A PEN WITH YOUR HAND and hold it tight. This was our relationship to God in the Garden of Eden. We had a tight relationship. We were created for a tight walk with God.

But we disobeyed God and chose to go our own independent way. Drop the pen to the floor. The fall was long and hard. Now we are dead in trespasses and sins. We can't get back to God on our own. We can't move because we are dead.

Salvation comes when we say, "yes" to God's offer to pick us up. He did (does) all the work by sending Christ to pay sin's penalty. Salvation is not a reward, but a gift we did not earn. Every religion is man's effort to pull himself up off the floor and make himself acceptable to God. Christianity is God reaching down in Christ and picking us up! Say "yes" to Jesus' offer of eternal life. He will pick you up and give you eternal life now!

Excellence from Ephesians 2:4-5

> *But because of his great love for us, God, who is rich in mercy, made us alive with Christ even when we were dead in transgressions — it is by grace you have been saved.*

Spiritual Warfare I

WE NEED ALL OF GOD'S ARMOR to fight the spiritual war we face. The belt of truth holds our uniform in place. The breastplate (chest protector) of righteousness protects our internal organs. Our feet are shod with the preparation to share the gospel anywhere and anytime. We catch the ball with the mitt (shield of faith). The helmet prevents injury from Satan's backswings, which would call into question our salvation. Every catcher must hit, and the sword of the spirit (bat) is the Word of God.

Excellence from Ephesians 6:11

Put on the full armor of God so that you can take your stand against the devil's schemes.

Spiritual Warfare II

ONE OF THESE HELMETS is brand new. What a thrill to put it on! The second is scraped and battle-scarred. It has been through the physical contact of many games. It is tried and proven.

It's great to be a new believer in Jesus. But it is the experiences of life that prove and mature us. It is victory in the conflicts and trials of life that brings great glory to the Lord Jesus and the Kingdom of God. There is no glory without a daily fight with sin and Satan.

We are headed in the opposite direction from the devil. If you don't experience daily conflict with the enemy, have you considered you may be moving in the same direction?

Excellence from 1 Timothy 6:12

Fight the good fight of the faith. Take hold of the eternal life to which you were called when you made your good confession in the presence of many witnesses.

Teamwork

GEESE FLY SOUTH for the winter in V formation. The lead goose breaks the wind and the others benefit from the wake created by the goose immediately in front. They rotate leadership so the lead goose doesn't get too exhausted.

An injured goose is not left alone to fend for himself. A healthy one stays behind with him until he's able to resume flight.

The honking noise of geese in flight is for a purpose. They are encouraging one another along. Scientists believe geese can fly 72 percent further together than they could fly alone.

The church is like a flock of geese. We really do need each other.

Honk! Honk! Honk!

Excellence from Philippians 2:1-2

If you have any encouragement from being united with Christ, if any comfort from his love, if any fellowship with the Spirit, if any tenderness and compassion, then make my joy complete by being like-minded, having the same love, being one in spirit and purpose.

The Cost of Sin

A Mathematical Formula

THE COST OF SIN IS INFINITE:

PERSON	X	LENGTH OF PUNISHMENT	=	PAYMENT FOR SIN
∞		1	=	∞
Jesus (being Infinite)		Died once for all		paid an infinite price

or

1	X	∞	=	∞
You (being finite)		eternal punishment in hell		will pay an infinite price

Who will you choose to pay for your sin? Will you accept Jesus' payment? Or will you eternally pay your own debt in Hell?

Excellence from 1 Corinthians 15:3

. . . Christ died for our sins . . .

The Holy Spirit

HERE'S A DEFLATED FOOTBALL. It has no integrity. How far can you throw a football? Can you throw this one that far? Why not? Because it has no air inside, it cannot do what it was designed to do. It can never be passed or punted as far when there is nothing inside. You can pull the sides out and try to make it look like it should. You can make it resemble its intended shape, but it still won't work.

When Adam sinned, he was deflated like a punctured football. We naturally sin and are deflated as well. We need to be supernaturally filled with the Holy Spirit so God can do what He intends to do with us and through us. Some people pull the sides out to make it look good, but nothing can replace the filling of the Holy Spirit.

Excellence from Ephesians 5:18

> *. . . be filled with the Spirit*

The Winning Run

PERHAPS YOU HAVE READ this book, but never personally trusted the Savior with your earthly life and your eternal destiny. The following baseball illustration explains how you can come to know the Lord Jesus Christ:

In baseball, a runner must touch all four bases to score a run for his team. The path to abundant and eternal life is very similar to the base paths on a ball diamond.

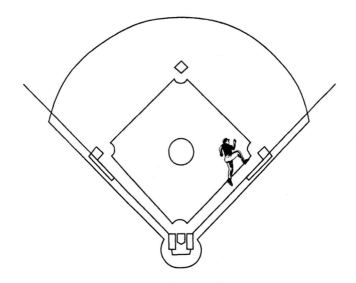

Step 1 (FIRST BASE) along that path is realizing that God cares about you. He not only created you, but He also loves you very deeply. He is seeking to give you an abundant life now and for eternity.

For God so loved the world that He gave His one and only Son, that whoever believes in Him shall not perish but have eternal life.

John 3:16

I have come that they may have life, and have it to the fullest.

John 10:10

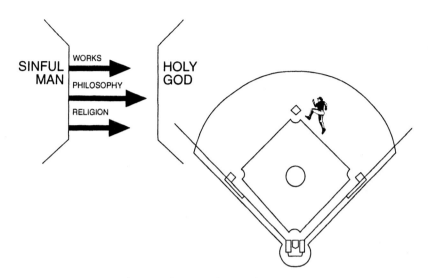

At SECOND BASE (step 2) we admit that we are sinners and separated from God. He is perfect, pure, and good; we are not. Because by nature we disobey Him and resist Him, He cannot have fellowship with us without denying His goodness and holiness. Instead, He must judge us.

Whoever believes in Him is not condemned; but whoever does not believe stands condemned already, because he has not believed in the name of God's one and only Son.
John 3:18

We realize we can never reach God through our own efforts. They do not solve the problem of our sin.

For all have sinned and come short of the glory of God.
Romans 3:23

But your iniquities have separated you from your God; your sins have hidden His face from you, so that He will not hear.
Isaiah 59:2

For the wages of sin is death, but the gift of God is eternal life in Christ Jesus our Lord.
Romans 6:23

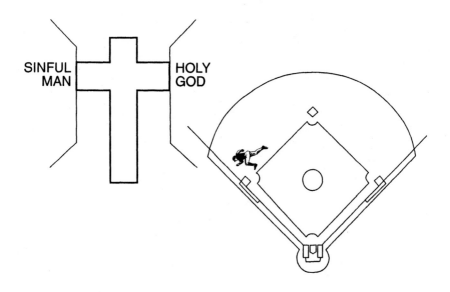

THIRD BASE is so close to scoring. Here (step 3) we understand that God has sent His Son, Jesus Christ, to die on the cross in payment for our sins. By His sacrifice, we may advance Home.

But God demonstrates His own love for us in this: While we were still sinners, Christ died for us.

Romans 5:8

For Christ died for sins once for all, the righteous for the unrighteous, to bring you to God.

I Peter 3:18

Jesus answered, "I am the way and the truth and the life. No one comes to the Father except through Me."

John 14:6

However, being CLOSE to Home does NOT count!

The Winning Run!

To score (step 4), we must personally receive Jesus Christ as Savior and Lord of our lives. We must not only realize that He died to rescue people from their sin but we must also trust Him to rescue us from our own sin. We cannot "squeeze" ourselves home any other way, and He will not force Himself upon us.

Yet to all who received Him, to those who believed in His name, He gave the right to become children of God.

John 1:12

For it is by grace you have been saved, through faith — and this is not from yourselves, it is the gift of God — not by works, so that no one can boast.

Ephesians 2:8-9

Why not receive Jesus Christ as your Savior and Lord right now? Simply say: "Yes, Lord," to His offer to forgive you for your sins and to change you.

_____
(signed)

_____
(date)

Tell someone of your decision and keep studying God's Word. These things greatly strengthen you (Romans 10:9-10). You may write *The Winning Run Foundation* for further encouragement. We would be thrilled to hear of your commitment! Welcome to eternal life!

THE WINNING RUN FOUNDATION
255B Settler's Road
Longview, TX 75605